# HOW ARE POSTCARDS MADE

## Cotton yarns for beautiful designs

The author has written two books on this subject, the second of which being this one. The first is a UK-based publication ''Handmade greeting cards'' (2021).

I'd like to dedicate this book to my Grandmother – Antanina M., who lived, resided and resting in Lithuania now, and thank her for the postcards she gave me.

*Nijolė Kavaliauskaitė – Hunter*

# HOW ARE POSTCARDS MADE

**Cotton yarns for beautiful designs**

by

Nijolė Kavaliauskaitė - Hunter

**Gotham Books**

30 N Gould St.
Ste. 20820, Sheridan, WY 82801
https://gothambooksinc.com/

Phone: 1 (307) 464-7800



Published by Gotham Books (June 27, 2024)

ISBN: 979-8-88775-945-6 (P)
ISBN: 979-8-88775-946-3 (E)

# CONTENTS

The fact that shelves in bookstores and other retailers are always being restocked is evidence of how popular postcards are today. They are more popular than messages sent by computer. Messages sent via computer are informational.  The image is reflected in the postcard, touches feelings and emotions. Postcards can conjure up fond recollections,  you can experience it emotionally and physically.  In order to spread the news, which has a pleasant tone; colorful cards can soar thousands of kilometers, across seas, and through an infinite expanse of the sky. As soon as you view a postcard, you begin to feel the emotions coming from the card. A postcard is like a newly acquired friend, or a guest who has just kindly knocked on your heart. There is no doubt that the content of the written message is sincere.

Postcards are simple to make, only desire and means are needed. My passion for knitting is evident in this publication. Why should postcards be drawn? They can be composed using various materials, combining into a means of expression which has nothing in common with each other.

# Essential Card Making Supplies

 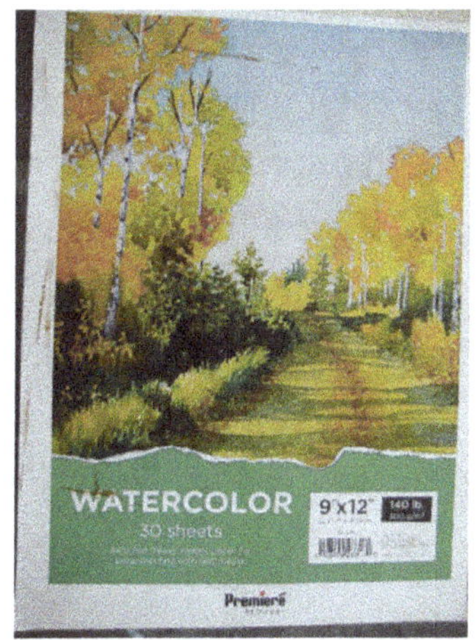


I chose *Paper* for drawing watercolors, it is not so thin, rather resembles a cute piece of cardboard, which, when folded in half, keeps the shape. Acrylic colors spread well on it. It's reliable as the foundation for components to stick to one another.

And *Cotton Yarns.* I didn't choose luxury ones. It is my belief that the content is revealed through color and the shape of the knit. The quality of the threads, in this case, was not a priority. As an inexperienced postcard designer, these yarns are the most plausible way to express an idea.

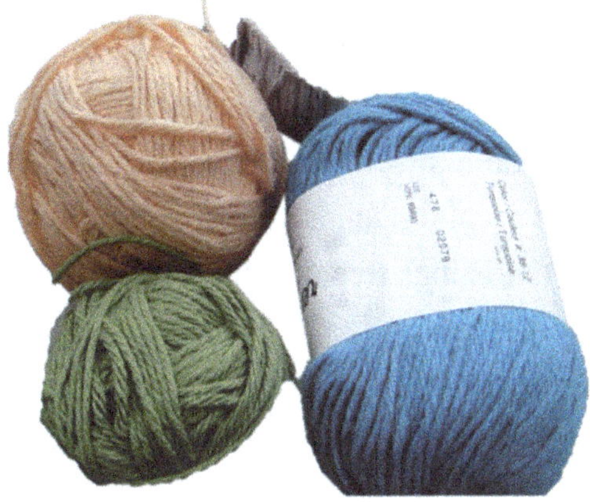

# How was the postcard put together?

Fill the background (paper space) with a specific color. You can color one or both of the folded sides; I chose to color one. The postcard is colored using a number of methods, which included light touches. You can also use a sponge. Use it to apply a thick layer of color on a blank sheet. If the light gaps between the colors remain visible, it is proposed to color a second time. Some postcards are painted in two or more different colors. On some, only light touches of colors are visible. All the elements in the postcard, including color, are composed to reflect an idea. For the sake of playfulness, I colored it without matching colors. There are three main colors: blue, red, yellow, but they, as a background, do not dominate. I chose warm and cheerful colors. One postcard was colored gray. This color is seriousness, peace, and in my opinion, respect.

## Knitted Elements

Various topics and techniques of varying complexity are displayed. You will see the examples of double (sock) knitting. You need three knitting needles. Some postcards are simply made using monotonous, repetitive knitted examples. I knitted flowers, which we usually give as a gift. The flowers are of varying complexity, done using various techniques. I love Christmas and have dedicated a few cards for this occasion. One of my Christmas trees is decorated with buttons. The second one is an abstract version of a Christmas tree. Rather than using a single, solid piece of Christmas tree, I knitted three colorful ribbons.

*Glue.* The knitted components must be joined with glue. I decided to use paper-glue-compatible adhesive.

I chose *Acrylic Paints*. When painting it, the result is quickly obtained via quick-drying paint. Their basis is acrylic resin. If thick, you can dilute it with water. After drying, they become resistant to the water, inexpensive and a wide selection of colors and shades to choose.

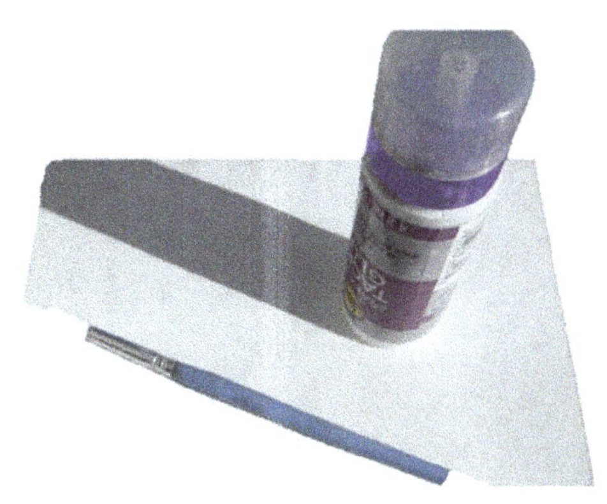

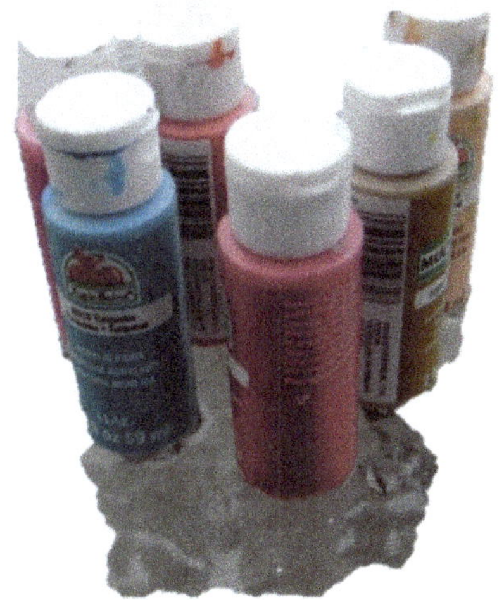

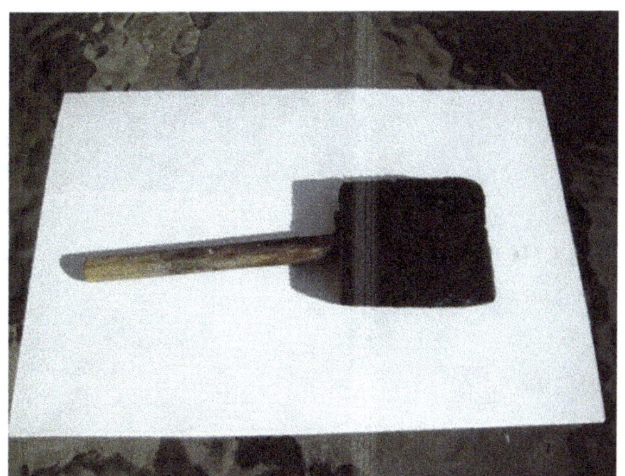

*Sponge*

## Knitting Abbreviations

To knit elements you have to understand knitting language, I mean abbreviations.

*Beginning and Ending of garment:*

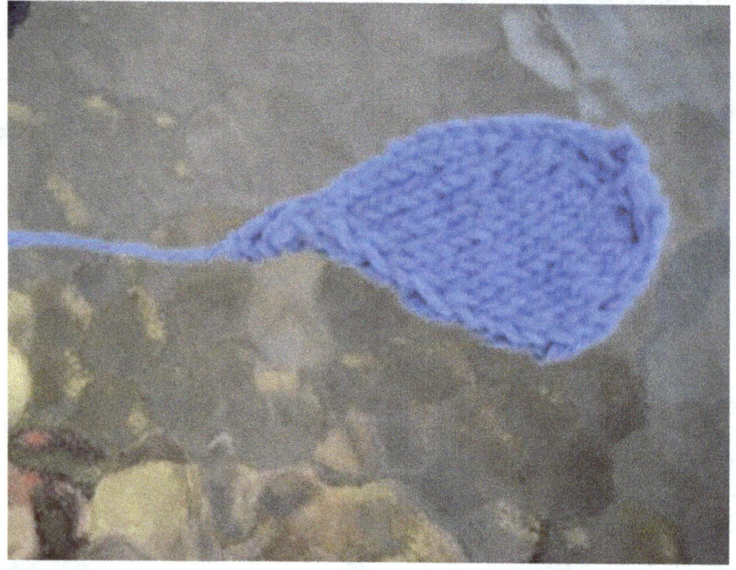

**CO** and **BO** mean "Cast on" (Beginning) and "Bind off" (Ending).

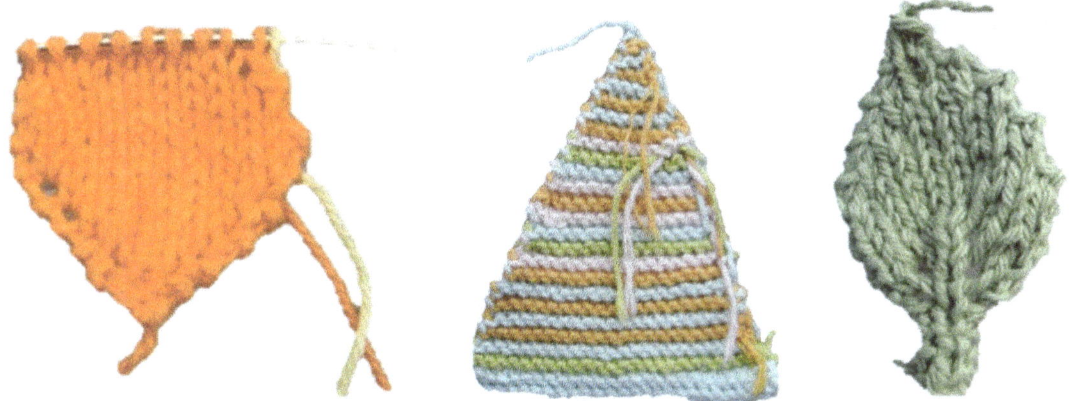

**RS** (Right side) and **WS** (Wrong side) of the garment. RS typically seems smoother. It is made with knit stitches. When compared to the right side/ RS, the wrong side/WS of the garment appears rougher, and single stitches stand out more. The knitted garment's wrong side conceals the ends of the cut yarn.


## Type of stitches:

**Knit stitch – K.,** (To make this stich you have to pass through the previous loop from below).

**K2** or **P2**, means "knit two stitches, purl two stitches". It was mostly utilized to make the garment smaller. Or it could be a component of a certain design.

## Area of Stitching:

**Tog** - means that the stitches should be knitted together. As an illustration, "k2tog" stands for knitting two stitches together as if they were one stitch.

**PSSO -** means "pass the slipped stitch over".

*Combination of stitches:*

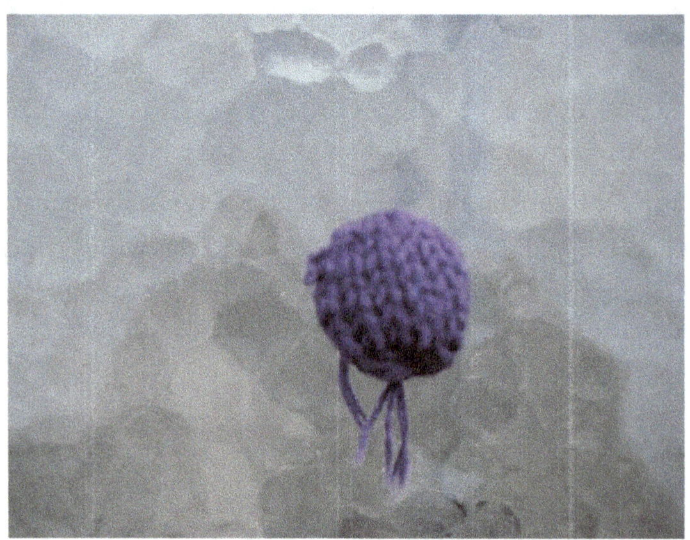

**MB** is definition for "make *bobble*". Bobble stitches need a lot of back-and-forth turning of your work, which might be scary at first. However, once you learn it, it's extremely simple!

**SMB - Five stitches Bobble.**

Knit 1 (keep on left needle), yarn over, knit1 (keep on left needle), yarn over, knit 1 in the same stitch (remove from left needle). Turn garment.

Turn your work and purl the group of five stitches.
Turn your work and knit the group of five stitches.
Turn your work and purl the group of five stitches.
Turn your work and knit the group of five stitches.
Turn your work and purl the group of five stitches.
Turn your work one last time and knit the five stitches together. The finished bobble should now be in the one stitch that is on your needle.

**9MB** - 9 stitches are made out of one stitch. Follow directions. Knit 1, yarn over, knit1, yarn over, knit 1, yarn over, knit1, yarn over, knit1 in the same stitch. Turn garment.

Turn your work and purl the group of nine stitches.
Turn your work and knit the group of nine stitches.
Turn your work and purl the group of nine stitches.
Turn your work and knit the group of nine stitches.
Turn your work and purl the group of nine stitches.
Turn your work and knit the group of nine stitches.
Turn your work and purl the group of nine stitches.
Turn your work one last time and knit the nine stitches together. The finished bobble should now be in the one stitch that is on your needle.

**S2kp** another decreasing technique is known as S2kp, which stands for "slip 2, knit, and pass the slipped stitches over the just-knit stitch."

**Purl stitch - P.,** (To make this stitch, you have to pass through the previous loop from above).

**Slip stitch - Sl.,**

**Yarn over - Yo.,** (To make a yarn over, bring the knitting yarn over the needle between two existing stitches on one row, and then work that strand as a stitch when you work your way back to it in the next row).

**Slip, knit, pass over – SKP** (Slip the next stitch to the right knitting needle as if to knit. Knit the next stitch on the left knitting needle. Insert the left knitting needle into the slipped stitch and pull it over the first stitch and off the knitting needle).

**Knit 2 together – K2tog** (To "knit two together" is just like making a regular knit stitch, but you work through two stitches instead of one).

**Knit 2 together through right slant – K2togrs** (Insert the right needle through the second to the first stitch on the left needle as if you are going to knit them.  Wrap the yarn, pull it through and slip the stitches off as for a regular knit stitch).

**Knit 3 together - K3tog** (Insert working needle into three loops at the same time and knit as one stitch. This converts 3 stitches into 1 stitch).

**Make 1 – M1** (Insert the left needle from front to back into the horizontal strand between two stitches. Knit the stitch through the back loop).

**Make 1 Purlwise – M1P** (Insert the left needle from BACK to front under the running thread, and lift it onto the needle. Insert the right needle into the front leg of the picked-up bar and purl it like a normal purl stitch).

**Purl 2 together – P2tog** (Insert the RH needle purl wise into the next 2 stitches on the left handle needle. Wrap the yarn around the RH needle. Pull the RH needle through the loop, 2 stitches together as if you purl one.

[   ] repeat episode in braces only

# Eight Leaves of Autumn

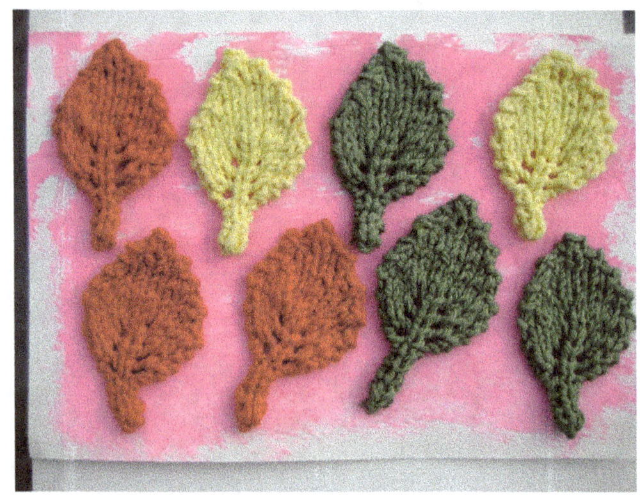

*When autumn arrives, the changing tree colors have an impact on the mood. They are transforming, shifting to a sad palette, and fading away. Focus your eyes on the beautiful colors outside. The hues of the season and the colors of nature fluctuate. This postcard captures the spirit of autumn. It mixes recurring element like leaves of various colors. It makes this composition simple.*

I used **Red cotton thread, Brown cotton yarn, "Sunrise" colored yarn, and the color of the "Tropical leaf"** to knit the leaves.

Two short needles are needed to knit the leaflet (suitable for knitting socks).

Cast on 3 stitches.

*Stem*
*Row* 1, 3, 5, 7(RS): Sl1, K2;
*Rows* 2, 4, 6, 8(WS): Sl1, P1, K1;
*Leaf*
*Row1:* Sl1, Yo, 1K;,Yo, 1K; (5sts)
*Row2:* Sl1, 3P, 1K;
*Row3:* Sl1, Yo, 3K, Yo, 1K; (7sts)
*Row4:* Sl1, 5P, 1K;
*Row5:* Sl1, 2K, Yo, 1K, Yo, 3K; (9 sts)
*Row6:* Sl1, 7P, 1K;
*Row7:* Sl1, 3K, Yo, 1K, Yo, 4K; (11sts)
*Row8:* Sl1, 9P, 1K;
*Row9:* K2tog, 7K, K2togrs; (9sts)
*Row10:* Sl1, 7P, 1K;
*Row11:* K2tog, 5K, K2togrs; (7sts)
*Row12:* Sl1, 5P, 1K;
*Row13:* K2tog, 3K, K2togrs; (5sts)
*Row14:* Sl1, 3P, 1K;
*Row15:* K2tog, 1K, K2togrs; (3sts)
*Row16:* Sl1, 1P, 1K;
*Row17:* K3tog; (1sts)

BO

Weave the loose yarns vertically through the rows. In order not to pull the fabric, work fairly loosely. Check the right side of the fabric to make sure that it looks smooth.

Soak multicolored leaves in lukewarm water. Avoid hot. Squeeze the water while easily squeezing them with your hands. You don't have to use my color scheme.  Choose yarn colors what is appropriate for you.

I used **Fuchsia** color to paint the postcard.

Color the postcard like you're drawing clouds with an acrylic paintbrush and a sponge.

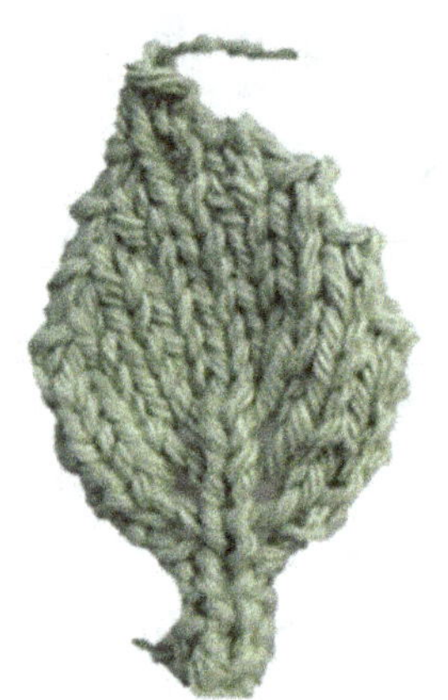

Once the knitted leaves have dried, spread the glue evenly across the knitted leaves. Adhere it.

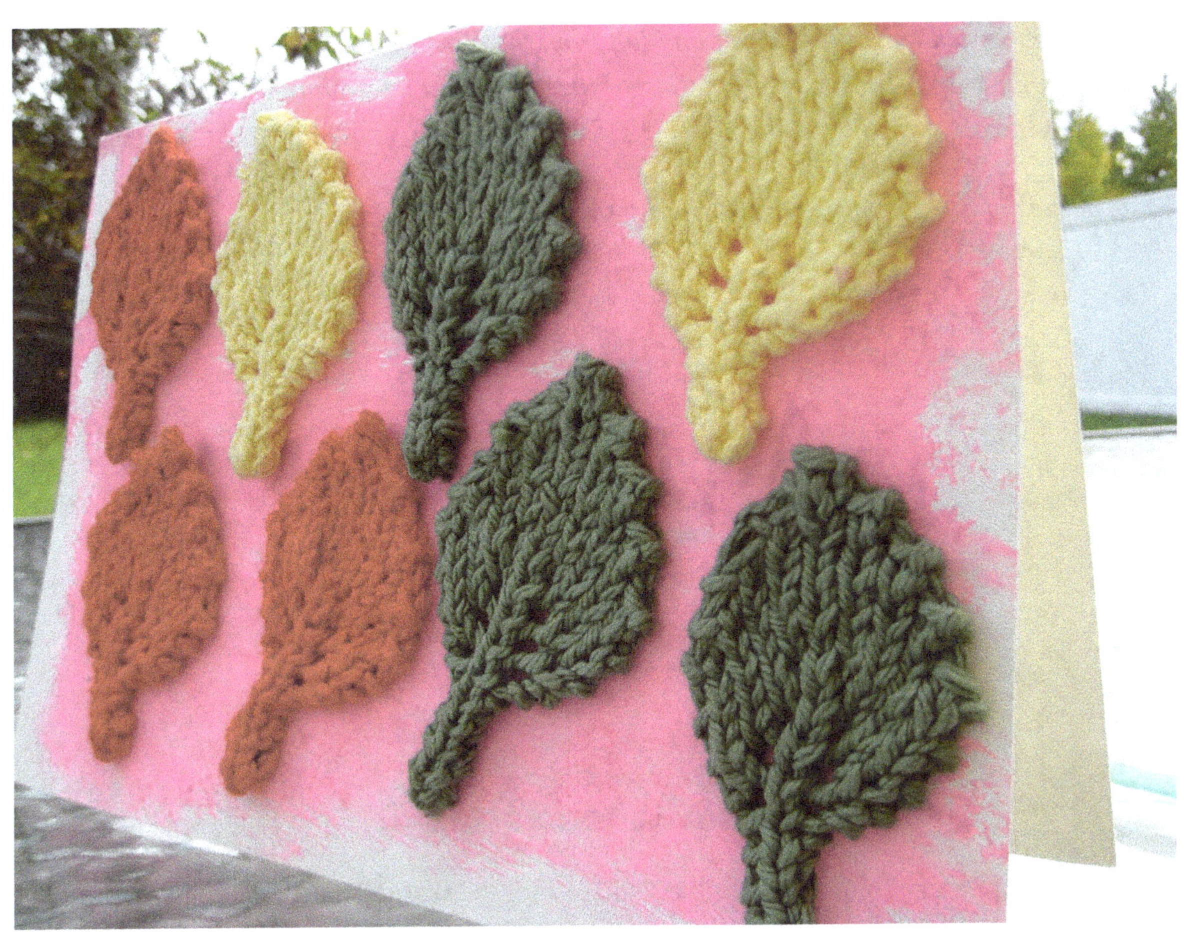

# Autumnal Trio

*Fall is the time when leaves turn color and fall from the trees.  They turn to brown and descend to the Earth for eternal slumber. They cling to the Earth and peacefully drift off to sleep.  The spring sun is awake now; they are no longer awake.*

*The memories of last summer are preserved forever in this bundle of leaves.*

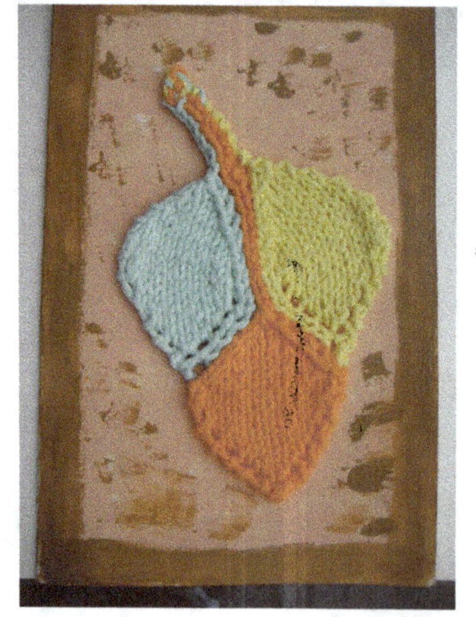

The postcard's primary color is **"Coral"** acrylic.  Color **"Caramel"** used to paint margins. The background with color **"Coral"** was painted loosely. The edges are colored lively; I did not aim for precision.

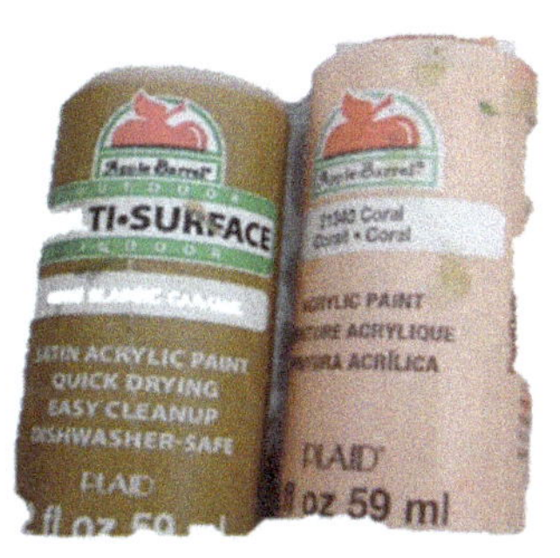

I used three yarn colors for knitting: **A - Orange, B -Yellow (Sunrise hue), and C - Mint.**

I use two knitting needles.

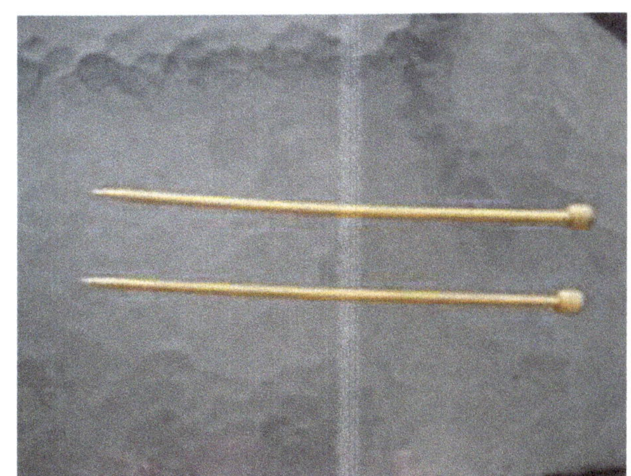

With color A, CO  2 stitches.

*Row1:* 2P; (2sts)

*Row2:* 2K, CO; (3sts)

*Row3:* K1, 1P, 1K;

*Row4:* Sl1, Yo, 1K, Yo, 1K; (5 sts)

*Row5:* Sl1, 3P, 1K;

*Row6:* Sl1, Yo, 3K, Yo, 1K; (7 sts)

*Row7:* Sl1, 5P, 1K;

*Row8:* Sl1,Yo, 5K, Yo, 1K; (9 sts)

*Row9:* Sl1, 7P, 1K ;

*Row10:* Sl1,Yo, 7K, Yo, 1K; (11 sts)

*Row11:* Sl1, 9P, 1K ;

*Row12:* Sl1,Yo, 9K, Yo, 1K; (13 sts)

*Row13:* Sl1, 11P, 1K ;

*Row14:* K2tog, 9K, K2togrs; (11 sts)

*Row15:* Sl1, 9P, 1K ;

To the main (**Orange**) color, attach a cotton **yarn of Yellow color - color B.**

Twist one colored yarn around another. You will prevent gaps and holes in your knitting.

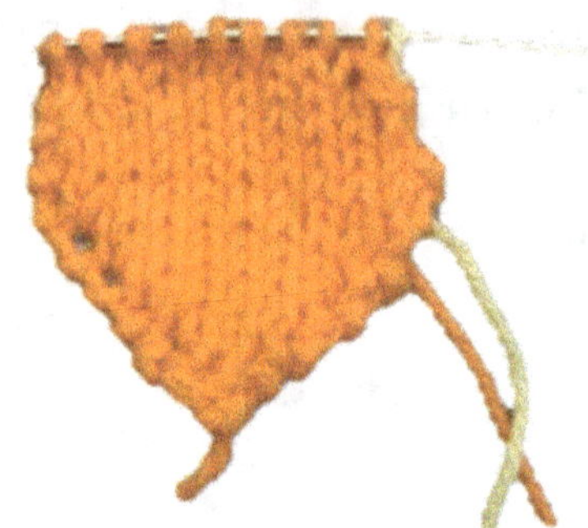

*Row1:* **B color** – CO (knit the stitch); **A color** - K2tog, 7K, K2togrs; **C color** – CO; (11 sts)

*Row2:* **C color** – 1P; **A color** – 9P; **B color** – 1K;

*Row3:* **B color** - CO (knit the stitch); 1K, Yo (3 sts); **A color** - K2tog, 5K, K2togrs; (7 sts); **C color** – Yo, 1K, CO;  (3 sts)., (total 13 sts)

*Row4:* **C color** – 3P; A color – 7P; **B color** – 2P, 1K;

*Row5:* **B color** - CO (knit the stitch); 3K, Yo (5 sts); **A color** - K2tog, 3K, K2togrs; (5 sts); **C color** – Yo, 3K, CO; (5 sts); (total 15 sts)

*Row6:* **C color** – 5P; **A color** – 5P; **B color** – 4P, 1K;

*Row7:* **B color** - Sl1, Yo, 3K, Yo, 1K;  (7 sts); **A color** - K2tog, 1K, K2togrs; (3 sts); **C color** – 1K,  Yo, 3K; Yo, 1K;  (7 sts); (total 17 sts)

*Row8:* **C color** – Sl1, 6P; **A color** – 3P; **B color** – 6P, 1K;

*Row9:* **B color** - Sl1, Yo, 5K, Yo, 1K;  (9 sts); **A color** - K3tog (1 sts); C color – 1K,  Yo, 5K; Yo, 1K;  (9 sts); (total 19 sts)

*Row10:* **C color** – Sl1, 8P; A color – 1P; **B color** – 8P, 1K;

*Row11:* **B color** - Sl1, Yo, 7K, Yo, 1K;  (11 sts); **A color** – 1K (1 sts); C color – 1K,  Yo, 7K; Yo, 1K;  (11 sts); (total 23 sts)

*Row12:* **C color** – Sl1, 10P; **A color** – 1P; **B color** – 10P, 1K;

*Row13:* **B color** - Sl1, Yo, 9K, Yo, 1K;  (13sts); **A color** – 1K (1sts); **C color** – 1K,  Yo, 9K; Yo, 1K;  (13 sts); (total 27 sts)

*Row14:* **C color** – Sl1, 12P; **A color** – 1P; **B color** – 12P, 1K;

*Row15:* **B color** - K2tog, 9K, K2togrs; (11 sts); **A color** – 1K (1sts); **C color** – K2tog, 9K, K2togrs; (11 sts); (total 23 sts)

*Row16:* **C color** – Sl1, 10P; **A color** – 1P; **B color** – 10P, 1K;

*Row17:* **B color** - K2tog, 7K, K2togrs; (9sts); **A color** – 1K (1sts); **C color** – K2tog, 7K, K2togrs; (9 sts); (total 19 sts)

*Row18:* **C color** – Sl1, 8P; **A color** – 1P; **B color** – 8P, 1K;

*Row19:* **B color** - K2tog, 5K, K2togrs; (7sts); **A color** – 1K (1sts); **C color** – K2tog, 5K, K2togrs; (7 sts); (total 15 sts)

*Row20:* **C color** – Sl1, 6P; **A color** – 1P; **B color** – 6P, 1K;

*Row21:* **B color** - K2tog, 3K, K2togrs; (5sts); **A color** – 1K (1 sts); **C color** – K2tog, 3K, K2togrs; (5 sts); (total 11 sts)

*Row22:* **C color** – Sl1, 4P; **A color** – 1P; **B color** – 4P, 1K;

*Row23:* **B color** - K2tog, 1G, K2togrs; (3sts); **A color** – 1K (1 sts); **C color** – K2tog, 1K, K2togrs; (3 sts); (total 7 sts)

*Row22:* **C color** – Sl1, 2P; **A color** – 1P; **B color** – 2P, 1K;

*Row23:* **B color** - K3tog; (1sts); **A color** – 1K (1sts); **C color** - K3tog (1 sts); (total 3 sts)

*Row24:* **C color** – Sl1; **A color** – 1P; **B color** –1K;

*Row25:* **C color** – Sl1; **A color** – 1P; **B color** –1K;

In order to knit the *Stem*, you need to repeat the 24th and 25th rows 15 times.

Knit the stem of the desired length. Cut off the tricolor threads. Pull them through one stitch on the needle (BO).

A bunch of knitted leaves rinse in lukewarm water. Avoid hot. Lightly squeeze water between your fingers.

When the knitted bunch of leaves dries, glue it on a colored postcard. Apply pressure.

# Dance of the Fall Leaves

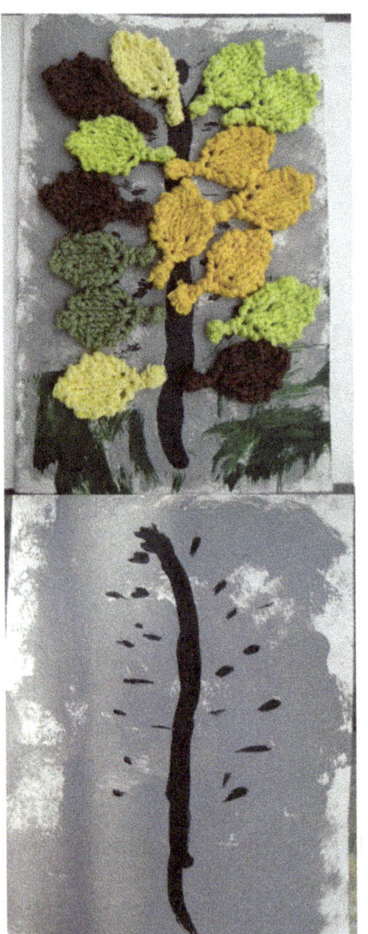

*To produce this card you need to knit tiny elements. The dark background, which is decorated with cloud-like shapes, reflects the dreary mood. The postcard's grey tone fades at the edges. The basic concept of the postcard is a tree, from which the theme is derived. The leaves on the tree have a variety of colors. It represents colors that it has accumulated over the course of the mature season.*

Three different acrylic paint colors are used to color the postcard: **Grey** acrylic color serves as the cards foundation or background. The grass is the color of "Tropical leaves, while the tree's trunk is asphalt-colored.

**Grey** acrylic color serves as the cards foundation or background. The grass is the color of **"Tropical leaf"**, while the tree's trunk is **Asphalt**-colored.

Two needles are used to knit the leaves. For knitting variegated leaves, the following colors are used: **Brown yarn, "Green lemon" yarn, "Sunrise" (yellowish) yarn, Rosemary (green) yarn, and Yellow-colored yarn.** Leaves are made using two short needles.

Put two stitches (CO) onto one needle.

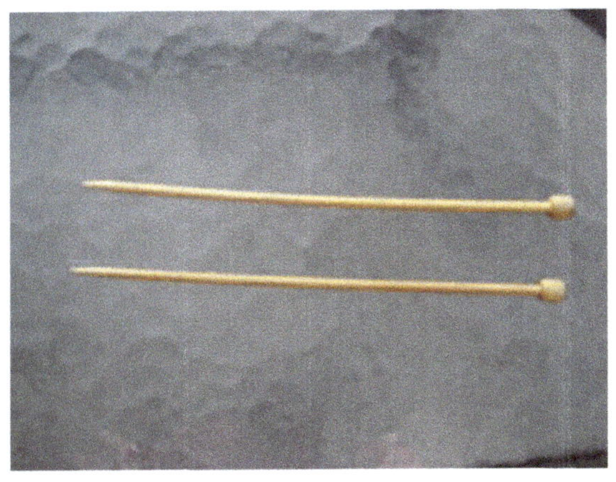 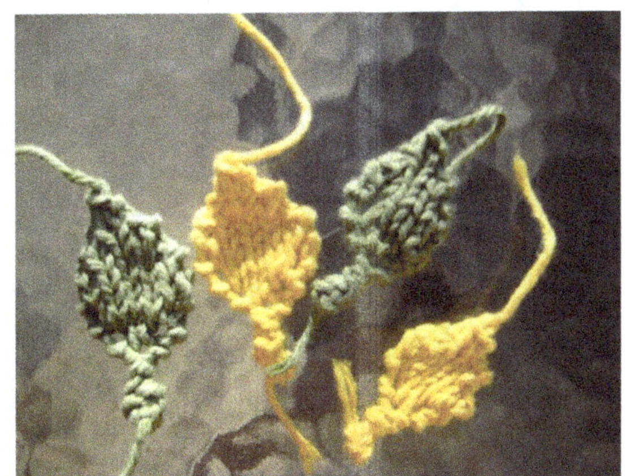

*Row1:* 2K; (2sts)

*Rows2 -8:* Sl1,1K; (2sts)

*Row9:* Sl1, Yo, 1K; (3sts)

*Row10:* Sl1, 1P, 1K;

*Row11:* Sl1, Yo, 1K, Yo, 1K; (5sts)

*Row12:* Sl1, 3P, 1K;

*Row13:* Sl1, Yo, 3K, Yo, 1K; (7sts)

*Row14, 16:* Sl1, 5P, 1K;

*Row15:* Sl1, 6K; (7sts)

*Row17:* K2tog, 3K; K2togrs; (5sts)

*Row18:* Sl1, 3P, 1K;

*Row19:* K2tog, 1K; K2togrs; (3sts)

*Row20:* Sl1, 1P, 1K;

*Row21:* K3tog ; (1sts)

Cut off the yarn and break it through the loop of the last stitch.  Hide the cut ends in the knit with the crotchet hook.

Moisten the knitted leaves in lukewarm water. Avoid hot. Lightly squeeze the water. Lay it on the soft surface to dry.

When the knitted leaves are dry, glue it on a colored postcard. Spread the glue evenly on the leaves and lightly press it to the surface of the colored postcard.

# Bonafide Friendship

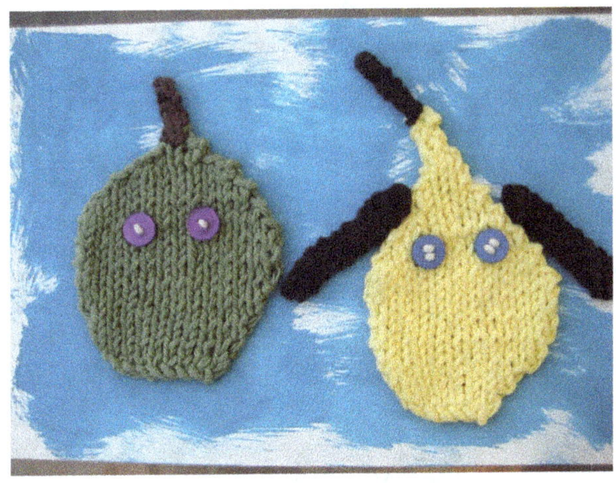

*Friendship is a real emotion that ties hearts together. Despite growing on different trees, these fruits met in the garden and spent the summer there swaying in the breeze, splashing in the rain, and in the sun. Autumn arrived, and their emotions grew older. Children, adults, cats, and even fruits can make pals. Friendship is a universal emotion shared by all living things, one that emanates from a pure heart. This postcard depicts the true feelings that occur when you become a friend.*

*Apple and Pear serve as the postcard's main design components. The pear signifies the female beginning, whereas the apple masculine beginning. It is a symbol of friendship between both sexes.*

The postcard's background is painted in turquoise acrylic paint with bold, jagged strokes and a white area that is apparent.

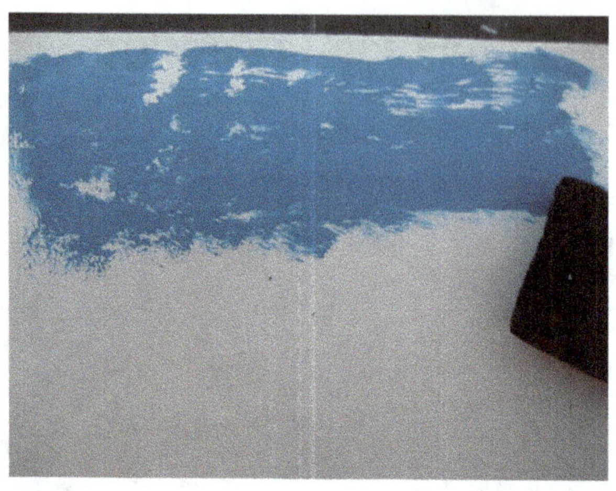

The vivid turquoise background draws attention to the elements that are arranged on the postcard's surface.

To knit Green Apple, I used **"Tropical leaf"** cotton yarn color.

Two knitting needles needed.

On one needle, CO 7 stitches

*Row1:* 7K; (7sts)
*Row2:* Sl1, 6P, CO; (8sts)
*Row3:* 8K, 2CO; (10sts)
*Row4:* 10P, CO; (11sts)
*Row5:* 11K, CO; (12sts)
*Row6:* 12 P, CO; (13sts)
*Row7:* 13K; (13sts)
*Row8:* Sl1, 11 P, 1K; (13sts)
*Row9:* Sl1, 12K, CO; (14sts)
*Row10:*13P, 1K; (14sts)

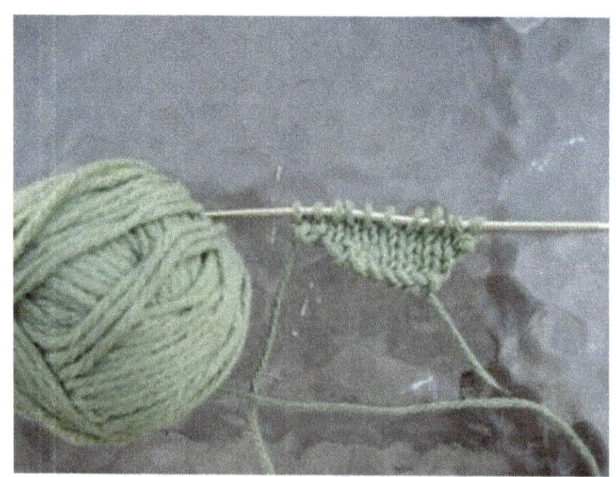

*Row11:* Sl1, 13K; (14sts)

*Row12:*Sl1, 13P, CO; (15sts)

*Row13:* 15K; (15sts)

*Row14:* P2tog, 12P, 1K; (14sts)

*Row15:* K2tog, 12K; (13sts)

*Row16:* P2tog, 10P, 1K; (12sts)

*Row17:* K2tog, 10K; (11sts)

*Row18:* P2tog, 8P, 1K; (10sts)

*Row19:* K2tog, K2tog, 7K; (8sts)

*Row20:* P2tog, P2tog, 4P, 1K; (6sts)

*Row21:* K2tog, K2tog, 3K; (4sts)

*Row22:* P2tog, 1P, 1K; (3sts)

Break the yarn, and attach it to a **yarn of Brown color**. Knit a stem for an apple.

*Row1:* K2tog, 1K; (2sts)

*Row2:* Sl1, 1K; (2sts)

*Row3:* Sl1, 1K; (2sts)

After completing the project, soak the knitted item in warm water and let it air dry. Sew buttons for eyes.

The **"Sunrise"** color cotton yarn is used to knit the Pear. There must be two needles. CO five stitches on one of the needle.

*Row1:* 5K, CO; (6sts)

*Row2:* 6P, CO; (7sts)

*Row3:* 7K, CO; (8sts)

*Row4:* 8P, CO; (9sts)

*Row5:* 9K, CO; (10sts)

*Row6:* 10P, CO; (11sts)

*Row7:* 11K, CO; (12sts)

*Row8:* 12P, CO; (13sts)

*Row9:* 13K; (13sts)

*Row10:* Sl1, 11P, 1K; (13sts)

*Row11:* Sl1, 12K; (13sts)

*Row12:* Sl1, 11P, 1K; (13sts)

*Row13:* Sl1, 12K; (13sts)

*Row14:* P2tog, 10P, 1K; (12sts)

*Row15:* K2tog, 10K; (11sts)

*Row16:* P2tog, 8P, 1K; (10sts)

*Row17:* K2tog, K2tog, 7K; (8sts)

*Row18:* P2tog, 5P, 1K; (7sts)

*Row19:* K2tog, 5K; (6sts)

*Row20:* P2tog, 3P, 1K; (5sts)

*Row21:* K2tog, 3K; (4sts)

*Row22:* Sl1, 2P, 1K; (4sts)

*Row23:* Sl1, 3K; (4sts)

*Row24:* Sl1, 2P, 1K; (4sts)

*Row25:* K2tog, 2K; (3sts)

*Row26:* Sl1, 1P, 1K; (3sts)

*Row27:* K2tog, 1K; (2sts)

*Row28:* Sl1, 1K; (2sts)

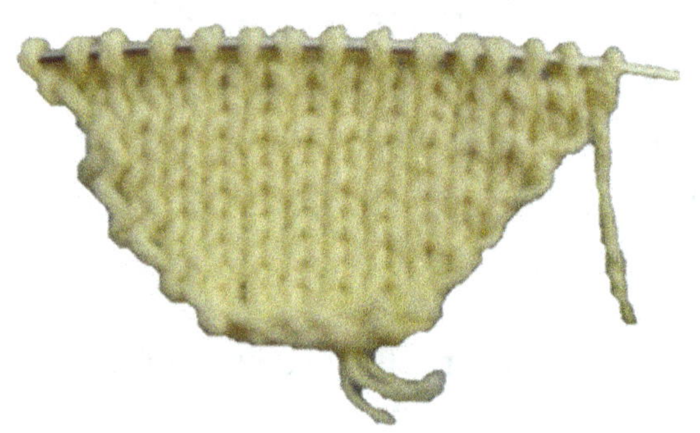

**Cut off the Yellow yarn and secure with Black. Knit the Pear's stem.**

*Row1:* Sl1, 1K; (2sts)
*Row2:* Sl1, 1K; (2sts)

Repeat 1 (first) – 2(second) rows 6 times. BO stitches. Cut off the yarn. Hide the ends in a garment. Sew eyes/buttons.

Hands of the Pear are knitted in black color.
Knitted with two needles. On one of them, CO 3 stitches.

*Row1:* K3; (3sts)
*Row2:* Sl1, P1, K1; (3sts)
*Row2:* Sl1 K2; (3sts)

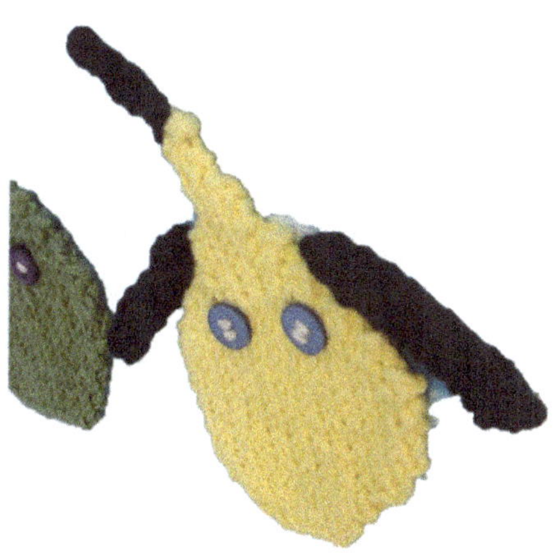

Repeat 2 (second) - 3(third) rows until you have desired length.

BO remained stitches, finish the knitting.

Hide the cut ends in the knitwear.

Rinse the knitted parts in lukewarm water. Avoid hot. Lightly pressing between your fingers, squeeze the water.

When the knitted fruits are dry, glue your projects on a colored postcard. Apply glue on knitted parts evenly. Attach the fruit to the surface of the colored postcard

# Cornflowers in Bloom

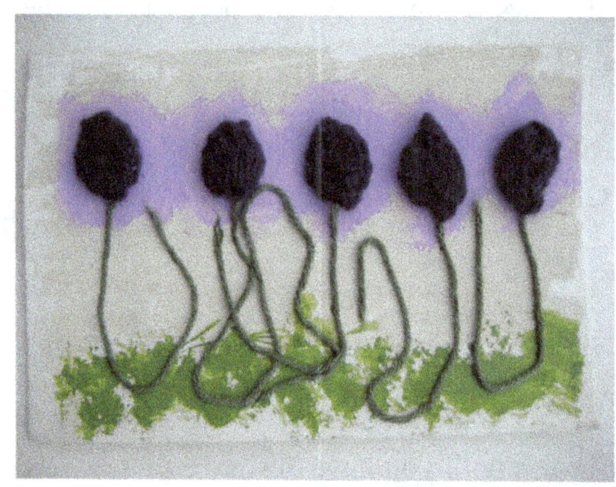

*When you see the Cornflowers blooming, which appears to be the Sky condensed into a series of flowers; you won't be able to take your eyes off them. The flowers are a representation of Heaven on Earth. You won't pass up the chance to show them affection while your eyes are fixed on them. The color is beautiful, so why even wind is so anxious and jealous. As the wind blows, the flower bends, but collectively rather than individually. They are clinging to the wind because Cornflowers aware must be strong.*

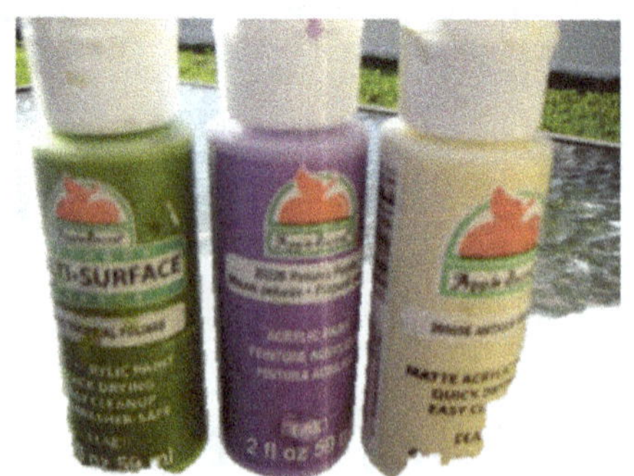

The color **"Antique White"** serves as the postcard's foundation. Apply it unevenly.

 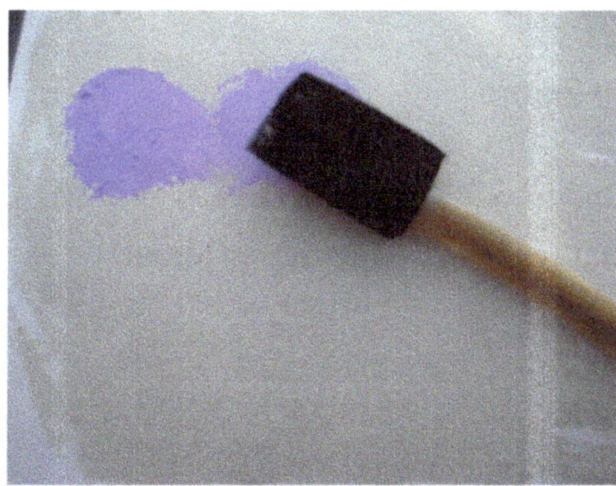

The Flower on the postcard was painted with **"Purple Petunia"** acrylic color.

**"Tropical Leaves"** is the color of the grass.

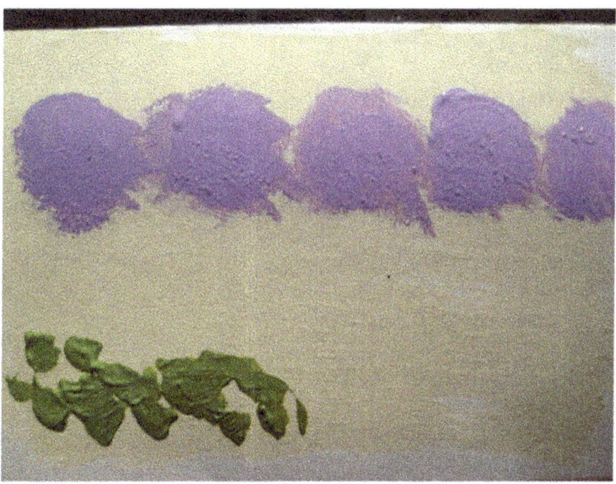

Making a card involves painting the card, knitting cornflowers, painting circles to attach the knitted flowers to, and finally adhering the cornflowers to the purple circles.

To paint grass, use thick dots of the color green.

Purple cotton yarns are used to knit the Cornflower.

There must be two knitting needles.

CO one stitch. In order to create extra stitches and turn it into a blooming Buddy, the main (initial) stitch should be quite loose.

9 stitches are made out of one stitch. Follow directions. Knit 1, but do not remove main stitch

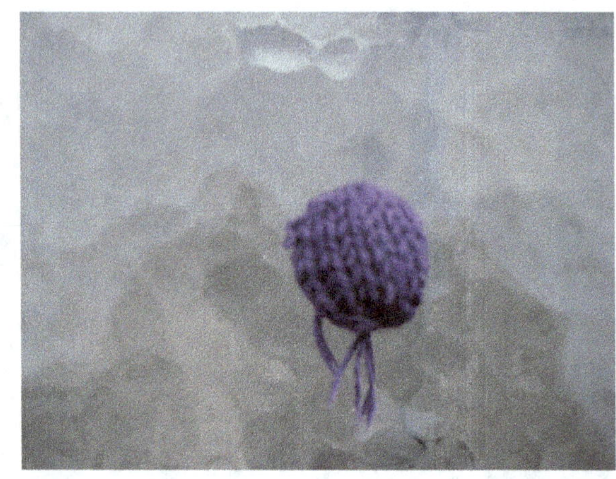

from the left needle (only new ones are transferred to the right needle), yarn over, knit1, yarn over, knit 1, yarn over, knit1, yarn over, knit1 in the same stitch. Remove from the left to the right ow.

Turn garment.
Turn your work and purl the group of nine stitches.
Turn your work and knit the group of nine stitches.
Turn your work and purl the group of nine stitches.
Turn your work and knit the group of nine stitches.
Turn your work and purl the group of nine stitches.
Turn your work and knit the group of nine stitches.
Turn your work and purl the group of nine stitches.

Turn your work once and knit the nine stitches together. There's one stitch left on your needle.
Thread yarn through the loop and make it tight. hide the free ends of the threads in a knitting.

To the end of the Purple yarn, attach the Stem of the Cornflower. Decide the length of the Stem and cut it off. Paint the grass on the card. Apply glue on a knitted Bubble/ Flower. Attach Bubble/Flower to the designated place on the card. Then circle stem/yarn in different ways, with a variety of curves.

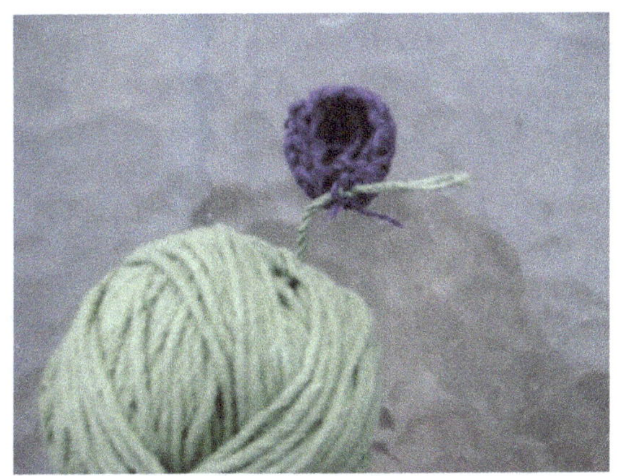
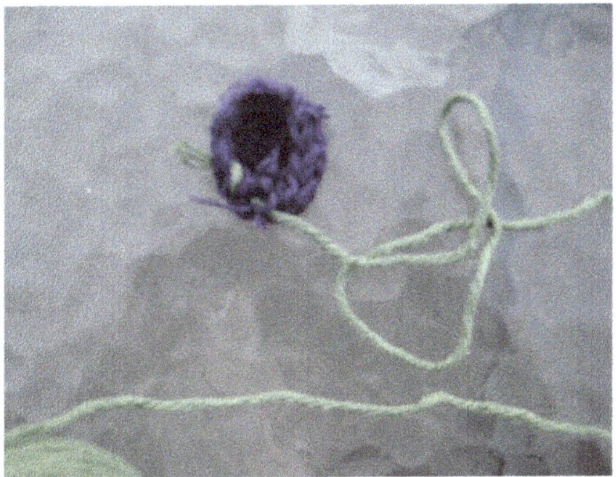

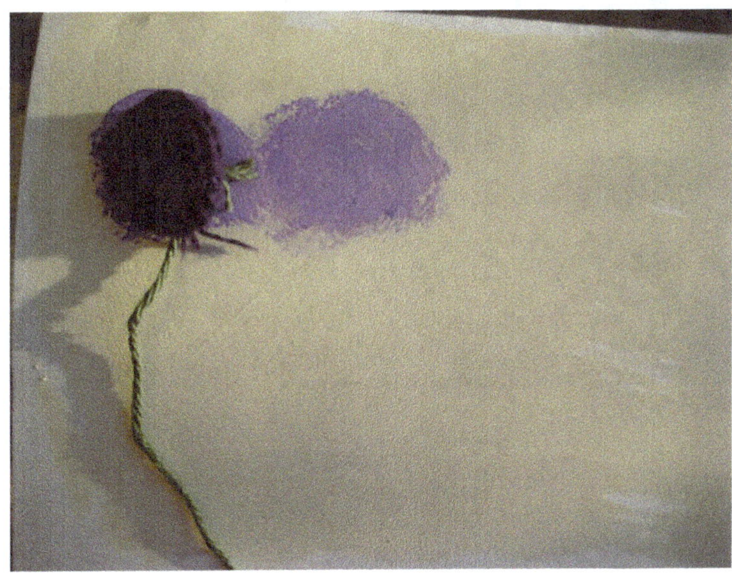

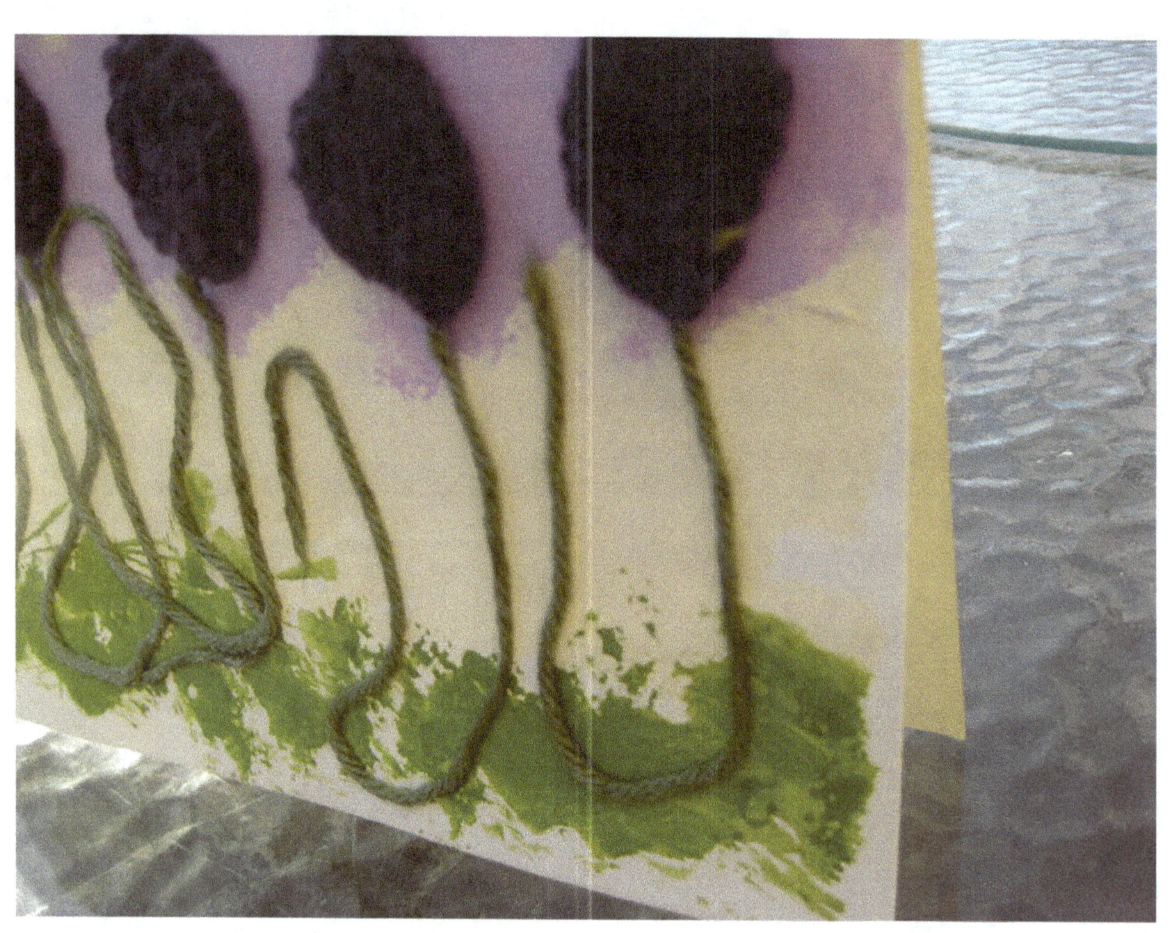

# Tulips in Bloom

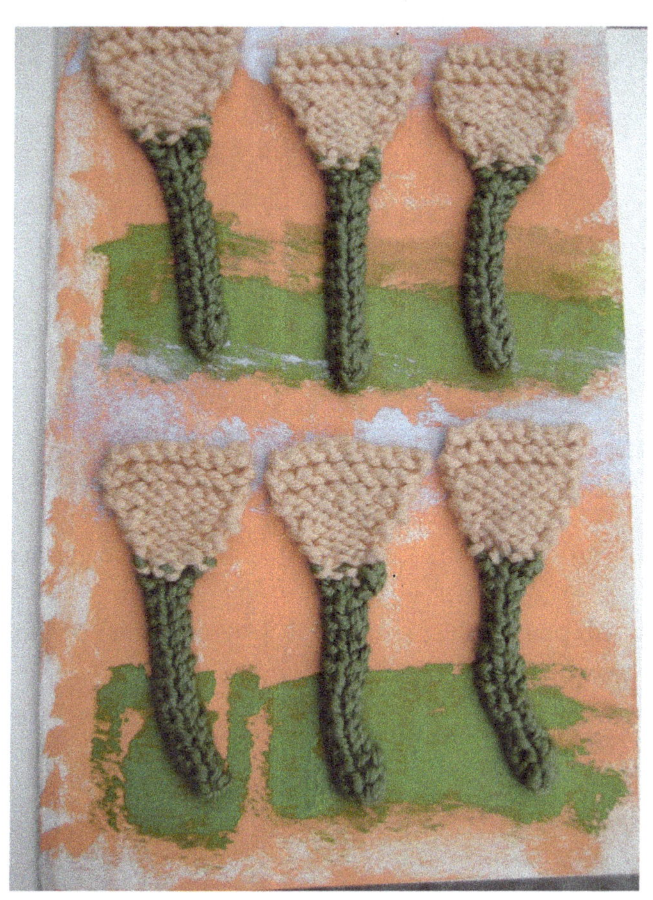

*The Tulip represents spring. The severe cold destroyed the basic elements of beauty, which spring has the capacity to reawaken. As one of the earliest plants to emerge, the Tulip gazes at the sunlight, soaking in its rays. Tulips blossom for a brief period.*

**"Tropical Orange"** is the dominant color of the postcard. The acrylic color "Tropical Leaf" is used to paint the grass. The spring sky's color is represented by the blue brushes.

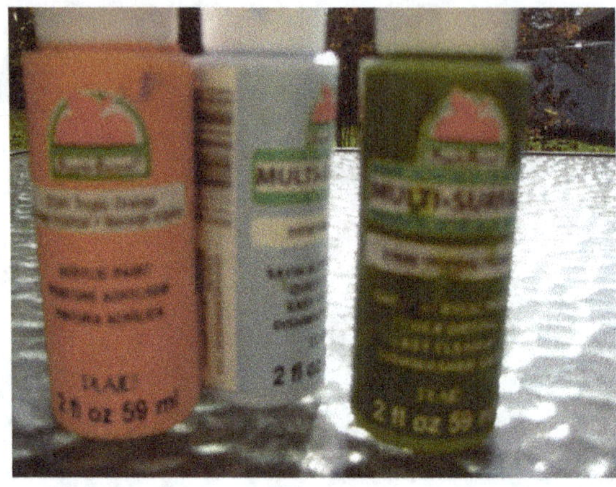

**"Tropical Orange"** acrylic color is used to paint the background of the postcard.

Do not completely cover card with paint. Leave white patches. Use green color to paint the grass.

Lightly touching with brush paint a clear sky. On WS (wrong side) of the flower, apply glue and glue it to the surface of the postcard.

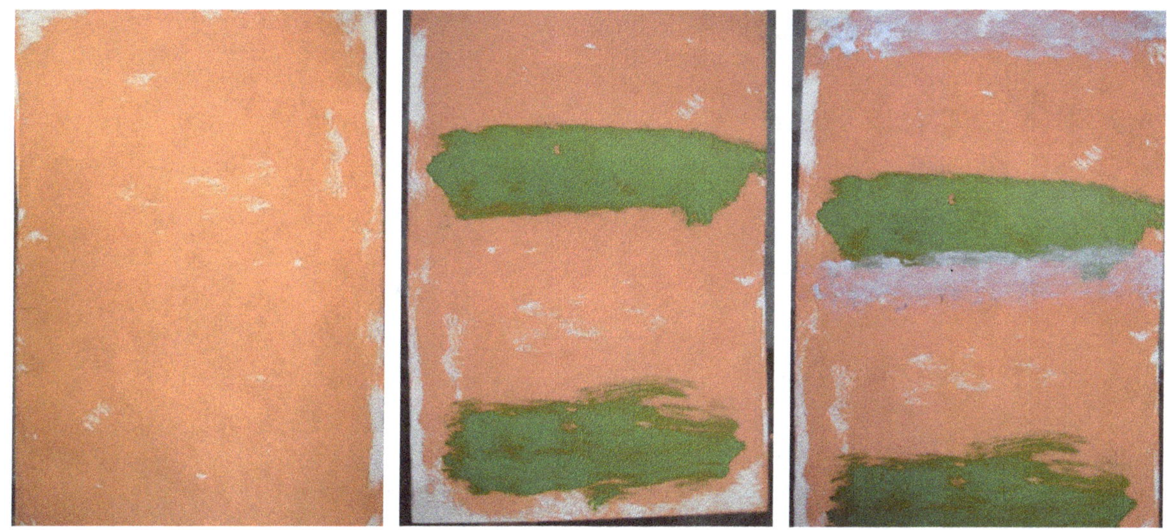

Use two knitting needles. Use **"Tropical leaves," cotton yarn color** to CO 3 stitches.

Knit Tulip's Stem first.

*Row1:* 3K; (3sts)
*Row2:* Sl1,1P, 1K; (3sts)
*Row3:* Sl1, 2K; (3sts)

Continue knitting in rows two, and three, until you have a 2.5 cm-long Stem.

The Green yarn should be cut off. **Tie a colorful yarn called "Tropical Orange"** to it. Knit Tulip.

*Row1:* Sl1, 1P, 1K; (3sts)
*Row2:* Sl1, M1, 1K, M1, 1K; (5sts)
*Row3:* Sl1, 3P, 1K; (5sts)

*Row4:* Sl1, M1, 3K, M1, 1K; (7sts)
*Row5:* Sl1, 5P, 1K; (7sts)
*Row6:* Sl1, M1, 5K, M1,1K; (9sts)
*Row7,9:* Sl1, 7P, 1K;
*Row8,10:* Sl1, 7P, 1K;

BO all stitches. Finish your knit.

Use a crotchet hook to hide the ends.

Tulips should be rinsed in warm water. Water may be easily squeezed between your fingers. Dry it. Place the wrong side against the painted postcard and adhere it with glue.

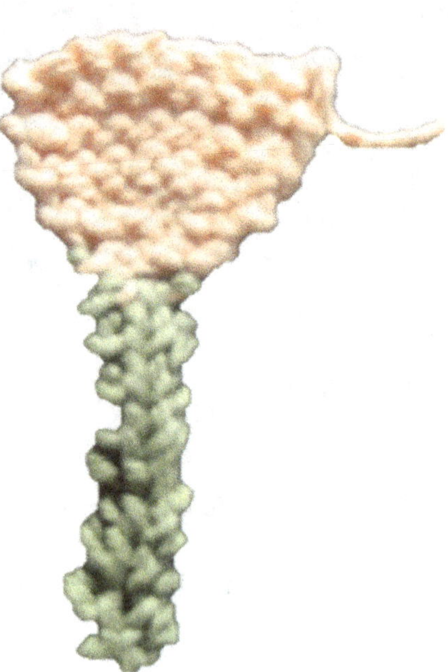

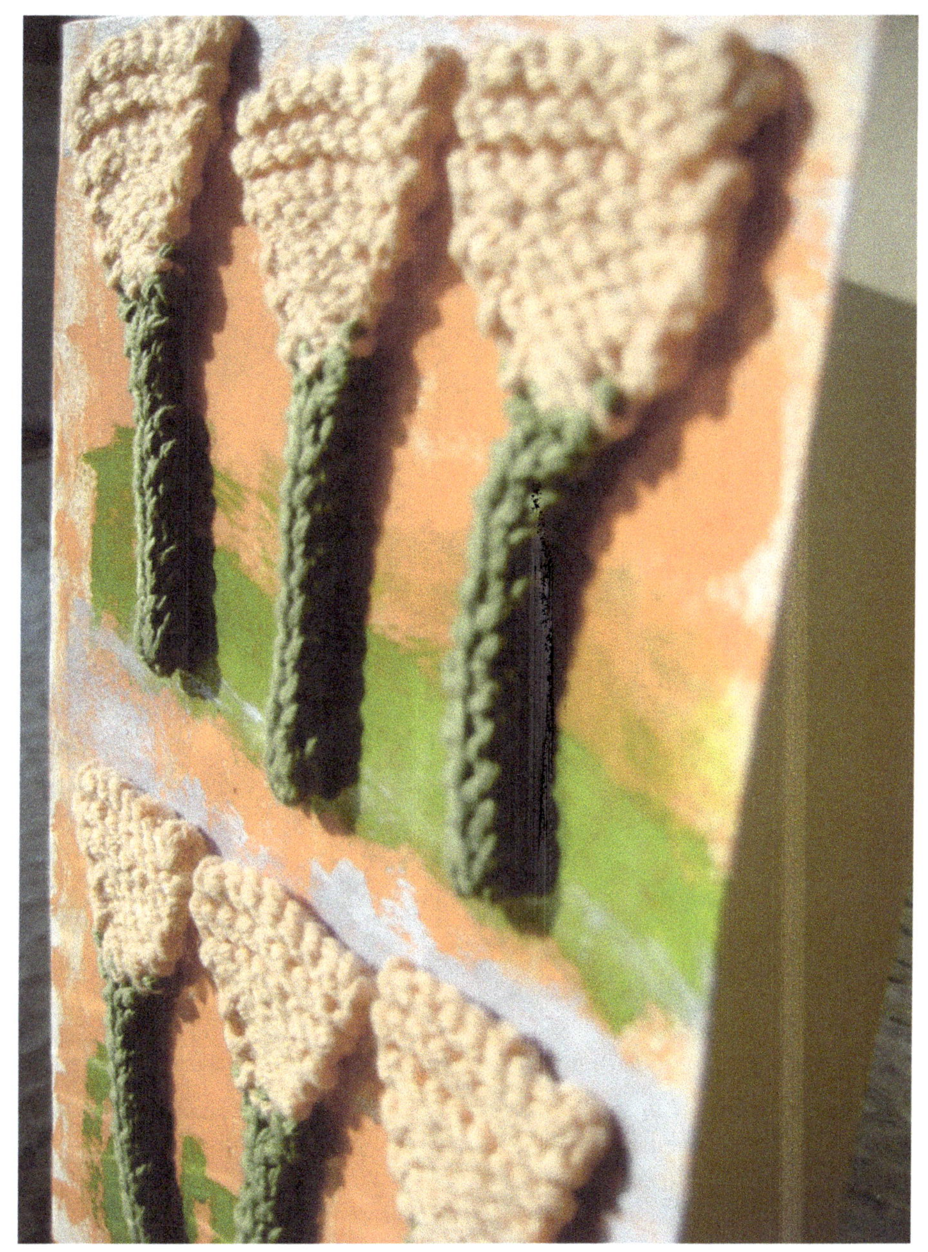

# Frosted Christmas Tree

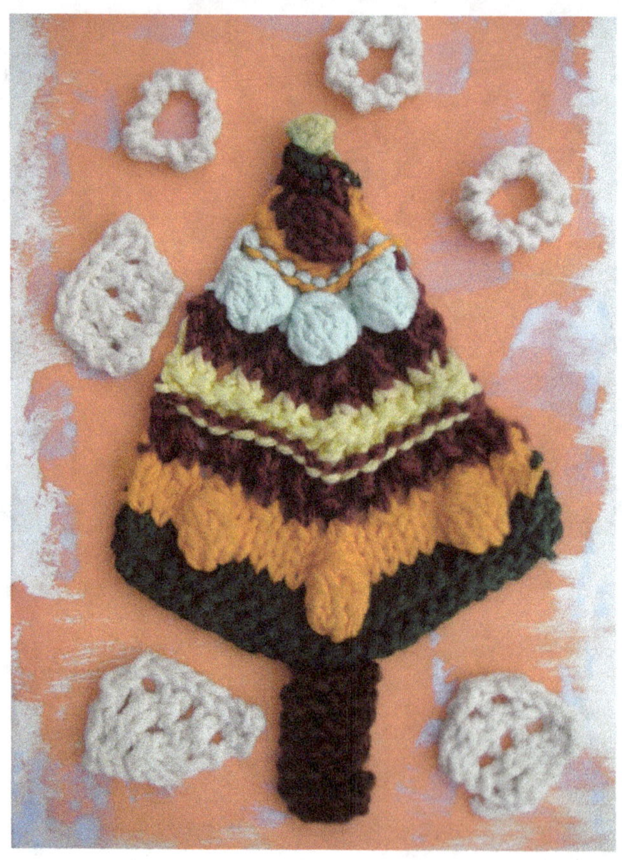

*The holiday tree represents joy. During a chilly winter, when plants and trees become naked, the Christmas tree gets illuminated in vibrant hues. It's decorated in accordance with one's heart's desire.*

Acrylic **"Tropical Orange"** is used to cover postcard.

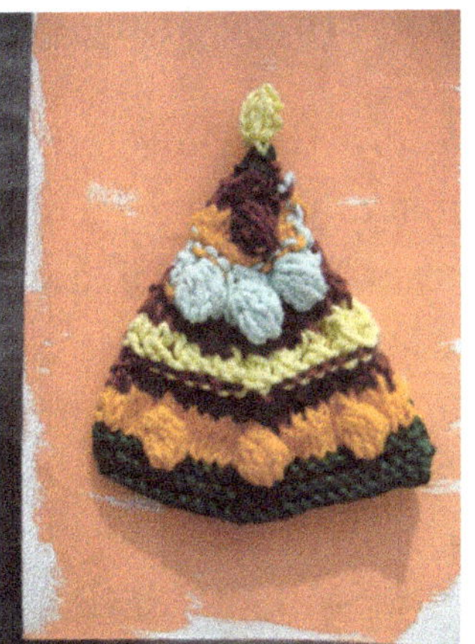

After the Christmas tree has been knitted and adhered to the card, **"Spring Sky"** acrylic color light brushes applied.

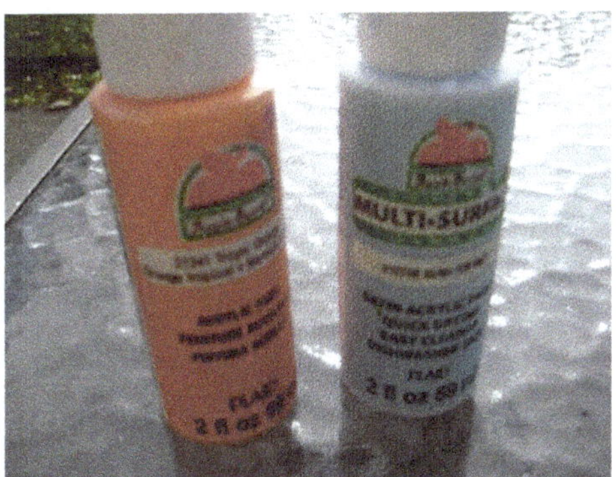

I utilized yarn colors like **"Sunrise,"** **Brown, Green, Orange, Wine, Mint,** and **White** to create a different knitting technique.

Christmas tree made using two knitting needles. On one of them, cast on 25 stitches)

<u>*Row1, 3:*</u> 25K; (25sts)

**Cut off the Brown color yarn, tie Orange.**

*Instructions how to tie two yarns together.* The two strands with tails pointing in different directions that are in front of you. Take the left tail and encircle the other yarn with it. Draw the yarn's tail from underneath. Bring the tail over the standing end to form a loop. From the bottom, pull the tail through the loop.

*Row5:* Sl1,10K, K3tog, 11K; (23sts)
*Row6:* Sl1, 21P, 1K; (23sts)
*Row7:* Sl1, 3K, SMB, 6K, SMB, 6K, SMB, 4K; (23sts)
*Row8:* Sl1, 21P, 1K; (23sts)

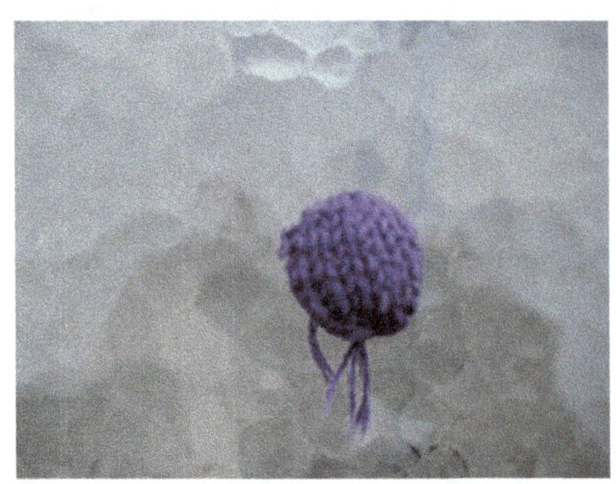

**Cut off the Orange color yarn, tie Wine – color yarn.**
*Row9:* [K2tog, Yo] rep 5 times, K3tog, [Yo, K2tog] rep 5 times; (21sts)
*Row10:* Sl1, 19P, 1K; (21sts)
*Row11:* Sl1, [K2tog, Yo] rep 4 times, K3tog, [Yo, K2tog] rep 4 times, 1K; (19sts)
*Row12:* Sl1, 17P, 1K; (19sts)

**Initiate the "Sunrise" color yarn.**
*Row13:* Sl1,7P, K3tog, 7P, 1K; (17sts)
*Row14:* Sl1,15P, 1P; (17sts)
*Row15:* [K2tog, Yo] rep 4 times, 1K, [Yo, K2tog] rep 4 times; (17sts)
*Row16:* Sl1, 15P, 1K; (17sts)

**Cut off the "Sunrise" color yarn, tie the Wine-colored yarn.**

*Row17:* Sl1, [K2tog, Yo] rep 3 times, K3tog, [K2tog, Yo] rep 3 times, 1K; (15sts)

*Row18:* Sl1, 13P,1K; (15sts)

*Row19:* [K2tog, Yo] rep 3 times, 3K, [Yo, K2tog] rep 3 times; (15sts)

*Row20:* Sl1, 13P, 1K; (15sts)

**Cut off the Wine-colored yarn, tie a Mint-colored yarn.**

*Row21:* Sl1, 5K, K3tog, 6K; (13sts)

*Row22:* Sl1, 12K;

*Row23:* Sl1, 1K, SMB, 1K, K2tog, SMB, 1K, K2tog, SMB, 2K; (11sts)

*Row24:* Sl1, 9P, 1K;

**Cut off the Mint-colored yarn, tie the Orange yarn.**

*Row25:* Sl1, 3P, K3tog, 3P, 1K; (9sts)

*Row26:* Sl1, 7P, 1K;

*Row27:* Sl1, 2K, K3tog, 3K; (7sts)

*Row28, 30:* Sl1, 5P, 1K;

**Cut off the Orange yarn, tie the Wine-colored yarn.**

*Row29:* Sl1, 2K, SMB, 3K; (7sts)

*Row31:* Sl1, 1K, K3tog, 2K; (5sts)

*Row32:* Sl1, 3P, 1K;

**Cut off the Wine-colored yarn, tie the Green yarn.**

*Row33:* Sl1, K3tog, 1K; (3sts)

*Row34:* Sl1, 1P, 1K;

**Cut off the Green yarn, tie a thread of "Sunrise" yarn.**

*Row35:* K3tog;

*Row 36:* Bring one stitch back to the left needle, and make a Small Bubble out of it.

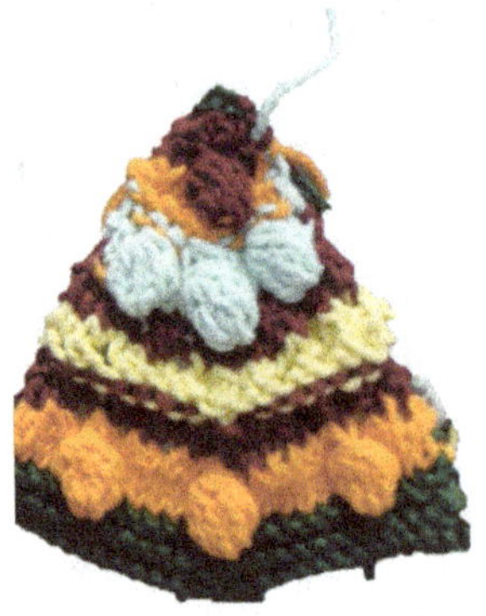

BO stitch. Finish the knitting. Use a crotchet hook to hide the ends in the knitting, hide all the cut ends of the yarn. Moisten in lukewarm water, squeeze the water between your fingers and dry it.

To knit the Christmas tree Stump, you'll need **Brown cotton yarns**.

On one of the knitting needles CO 5 stitches.

*Row1:* 5K; (5sts)
*Row2:* Sl1, 4K;
Repeat Rows 1- 2 four more times.
Knit decorations: Snowflakes and Snowballs.

**White cotton yarns** needed.

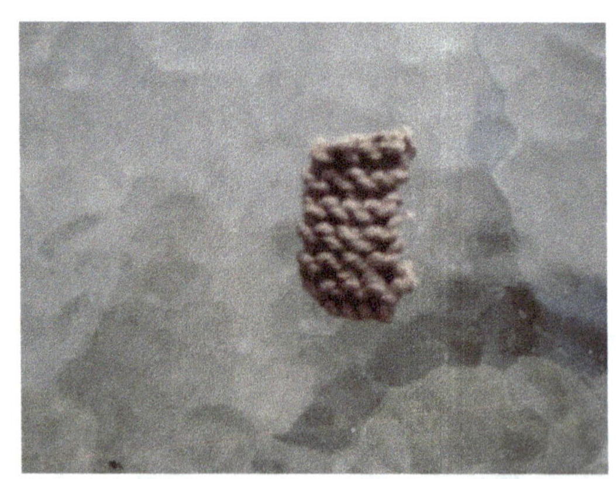

Two knitting needles, size 6 are required.
Making *Hollow Snowflakes*.
On one of knitting needles CO 2 stitches.
*Row1:* 2K; (2sts)

*Row2:* Sl1,1K, turn knitted piece, repeat this pattern (Sl1, K1) until this piece comes 1-inch long. BO (bind off).

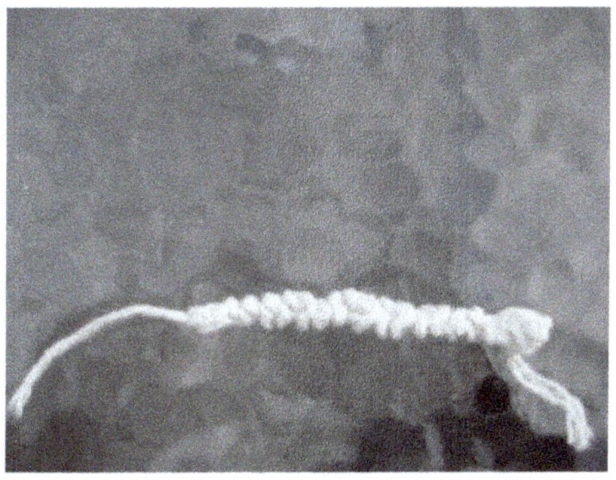

Connect the ends of the ribbon by sewing them together. Hide loose ends.

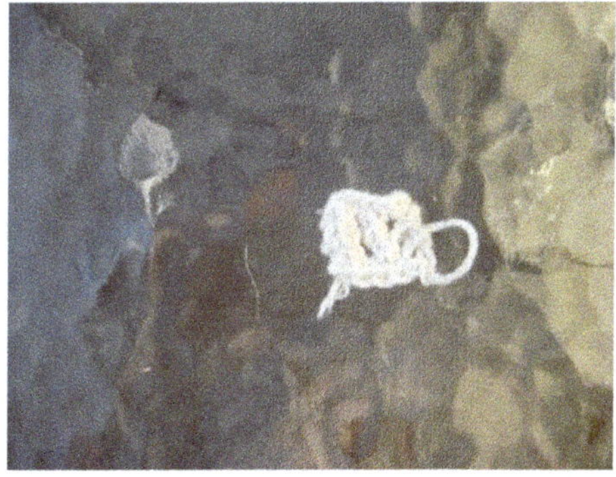

*Snow Balls*

Cast On 6 stitches.

*Row1:* 5P, 1K; (6sts)
*Row2:* Sl1, K2tog, Yo, K2tog, Yo, 1K;
*Row3:* Sl1, 4P, 1K; (6sts)

*Row4:* Sl1, K2tog, Yo, K2tog, Yo, 1K;
*Row5:* Sl1, 4P, 1K; (6sts)

Complete the knitting by binding off stitches.

Attach all knitted elements to the card using glue.

Paint with sky blue color acrylic. Improvise creating frosty impression.

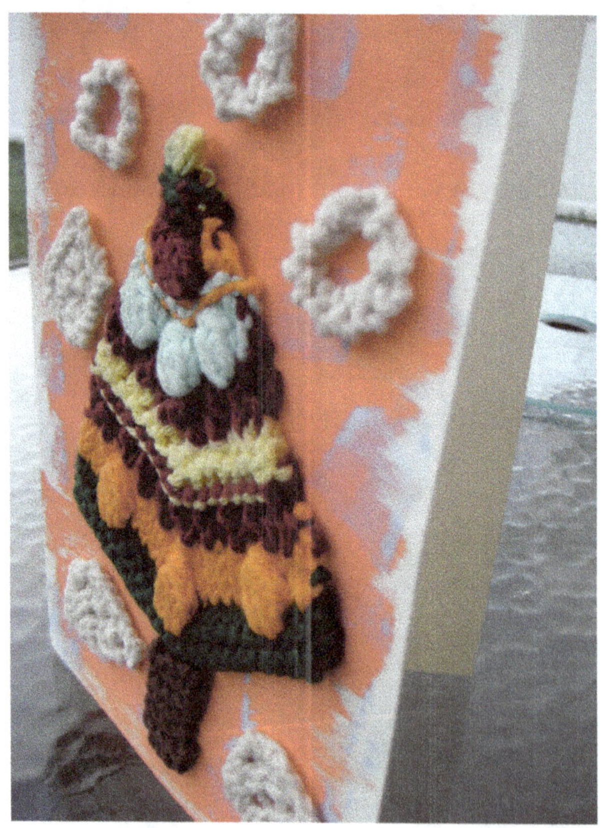

# Christmas Tree

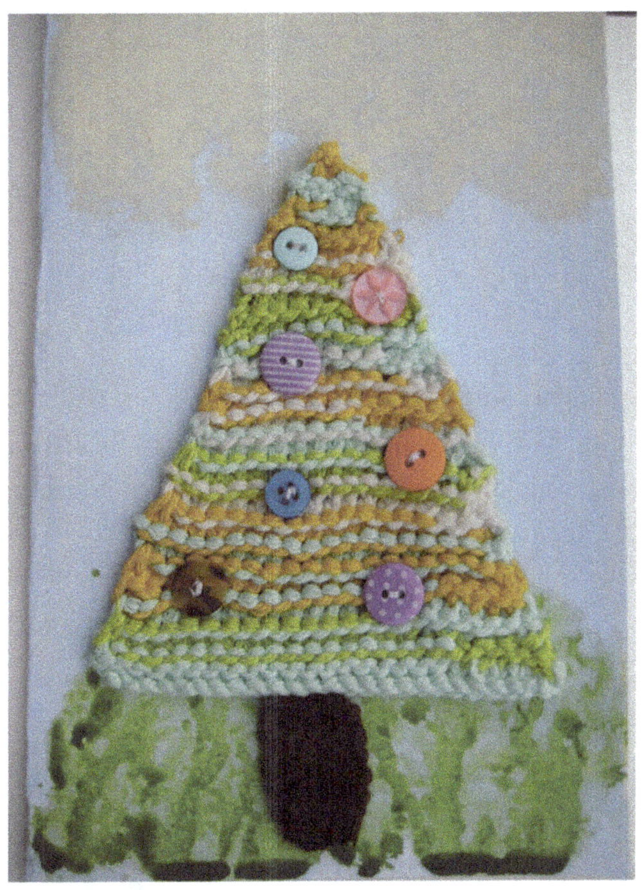

*Warm color combinations make up the stripes on the Christmas tree. Buttons are used as decorations. Even the top of Christmas tree itself aspires for the Heaven since it is so tall.*

The postcard is painted using "Spring Sky" acrylic color, with a sponge swooping down from above.  The clouds are painted in white. For the growth of the trunk, some grass is painted, just lightly splattering with wet paint to give the appearance that it is dripping.

Knitted with two knitting needles. CO 28 stitches on a one needle. I used **"Mint" -color cotton yarns.**

*Row1(Wrong side):* 28K;
*Row2(Right side):* Sl1, 27K;
To the main – **"Mint" colored yarn**, tie the yarn of **"Green lemon" color**.
*Instructions how to tie yarns together.* The two strands with tails pointing in different directions that are in front of you. Take the left tail and encircle the other yarn with it. Draw the yarn's tail  through the loop.
*Row3:* K2tog, 24K, K2togrs; (26sts)

*Row4:* Sl1, 25K;

Knitt with **"Mint"- colored cotton yarns.**

*Row5:* K2tog, 22K, K2togrs; (24sts)

*Row6:* Sl1, 23K;

Tie **Yellow color yarns.**

*Rows7, 8:* Sl1, 23K; (24sts)

Knitt with **,'Mint"- colored cotton yarns**

*Row9:* K2tog, 20K, K2togrs; (22sts)

*Row10:* Sl1, 21K;

Knit with **Yellow color yarns.**

*Rows11 - 12:* Sl1, 21K; (22sts)

Knitt with **"Mint"- colored cotton yarns.**

*Row13:* K2tog, 18K, K2togrs; (20sts)

*Row14:* Sl1, 19K;

Knit with **Yellow color yarns.**

*Rows15 - 16:* Sl1, 19K; (20sts)

To the main color tie cotton **yarns of White color.**

*Row17:* K2tog, 16K, K2togrs; (18sts)

*Row18:* Sl1, 17K;

Knit with **Yellow color yarns.**

*Rows19 - 20:* Sl1, 17K; (18sts)

Knitt with**"Mint"- colored cotton yarns.**

*Row21:* K2tog, 14K, K2togrs; (16sts)

*Row22:* Sl1, 15K;

Knit with **White color yarns.**

*Rows23 - 24:* Sl1, 15K; (16sts)

Knit with **Yellow color yarns.**

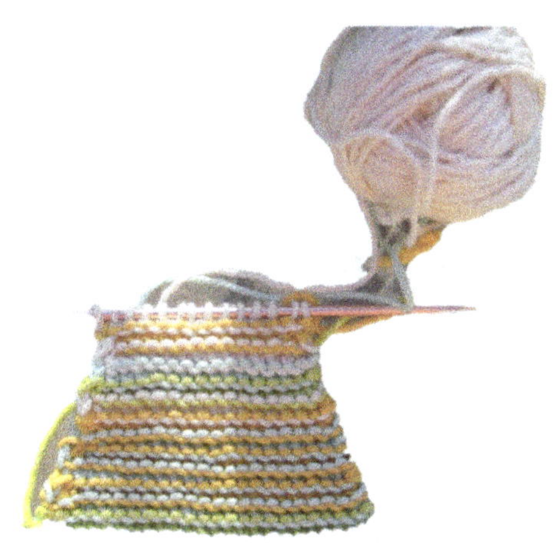

*Row25:* K2tog, 12K, K2togrs; (14sts)

*Row26:* Sl1, 13K;

Knit with **White color cotton yarn**.

*Rows27 - 28:* Sl1, 13K; (14sts)

Change yarrn to**"Mint"- color cotton yarn**.

*Row29:* K2tog, 10K, K2togrs; (12sts)

*Row30:* Sl1, 11K;

Knit with **"Green lemon" color cotton yarn**.

*Rows31 - 32:* Sl1, 11K; (12sts)

Knit with **White color cotton yarn**.

*Row33:* K2tog, 8K, K2togrs; (10sts)

*Row34:* Sl1, 9K;

Knit with **Yellow color yarns**.

*Rows35 - 36:* Sl1, 9K; (10sts)

Change yarrn to**"Mint"- color cotton yarn**.

*Row37:* K2tog, 6K, K2togrs; (8sts)

*Row38:* Sl1, 7K;

Knit with **Yellow color yarns**.

*Rows39 – 40:* Sl1, 7K; (8sts)

Change yarrn to**"Mint"- color cotton yarn**.

*Row41:* K2tog, 4K, K2togrs; (6sts)

*Row42:* Sl1, 5K;

Knit with **Yellow color yarns**.

*Rows43 – 44:* Sl1, 5K; (6sts)

Change yarrn to**"Mint"- color cotton yarn**.

*Row45:* K2tog, 2K, K2togrs; (4sts)

*Row46:* Sl1, 3K;

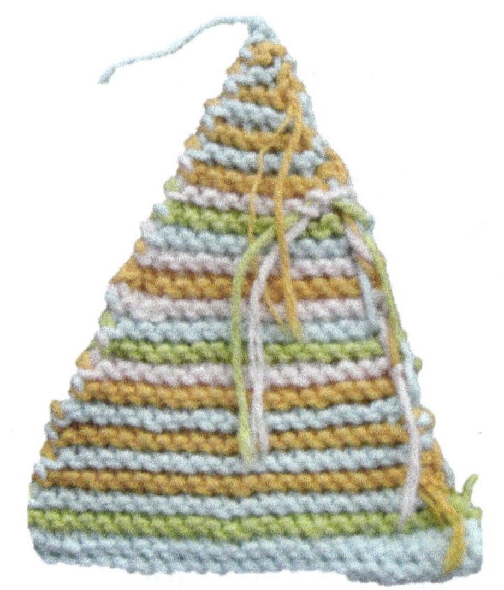

Knit with **Yellow color yarns**.

*Rows47 – 48:* Sl1, 3K; (4sts)

Change yarrn to**"Mint"- color cotton yarn.**

*Row49:* K2tog, K2togrs; (2sts)

*Row50:* Sl1, 1K;

*Row51:* K2tog, (1sts)

Complete the knitting by cutting off the yarns. Hide the yarn ends in a knit. Wet in lukewarm water, and after forming the shape of the Christmas tree, let it dry on the blanket.
Sew multi-colored buttons.

Glue to a colored and dried postcard.

*Stump* of Christmas tree
With **Brown cotton yarn** cast on 5 stitches.

*Row1:* 5K; (5sts)

*Row2:* Sl1, 3P, 1K;

*Row3:* Sl1, 4K;

Repeat 2 (second) -3 (third) rows 10 more times. Bind off removing all stitches from the needle. Hide the ends of the yarn in the knitting. Glue to the card.

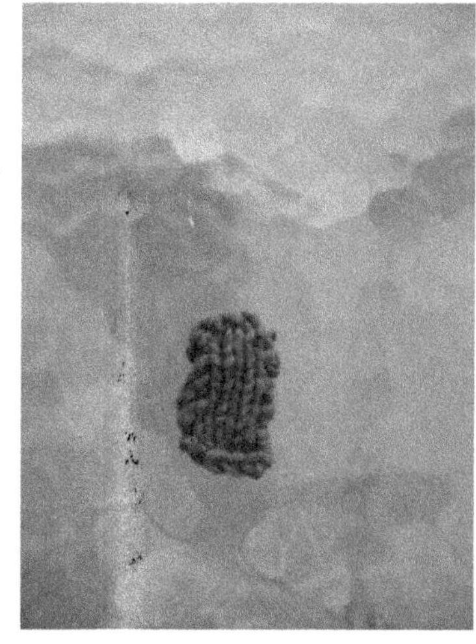

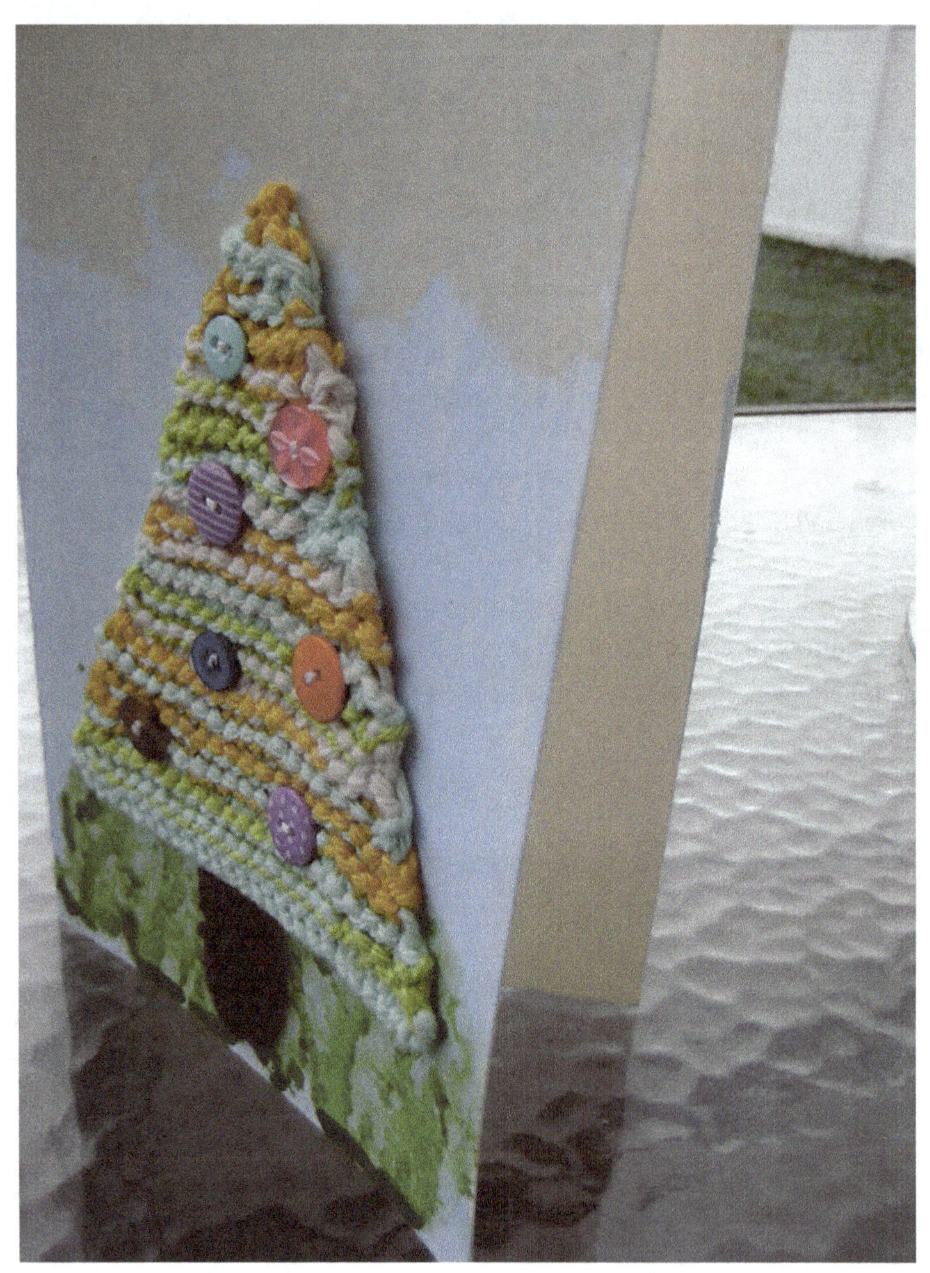

# Christmas Tree II

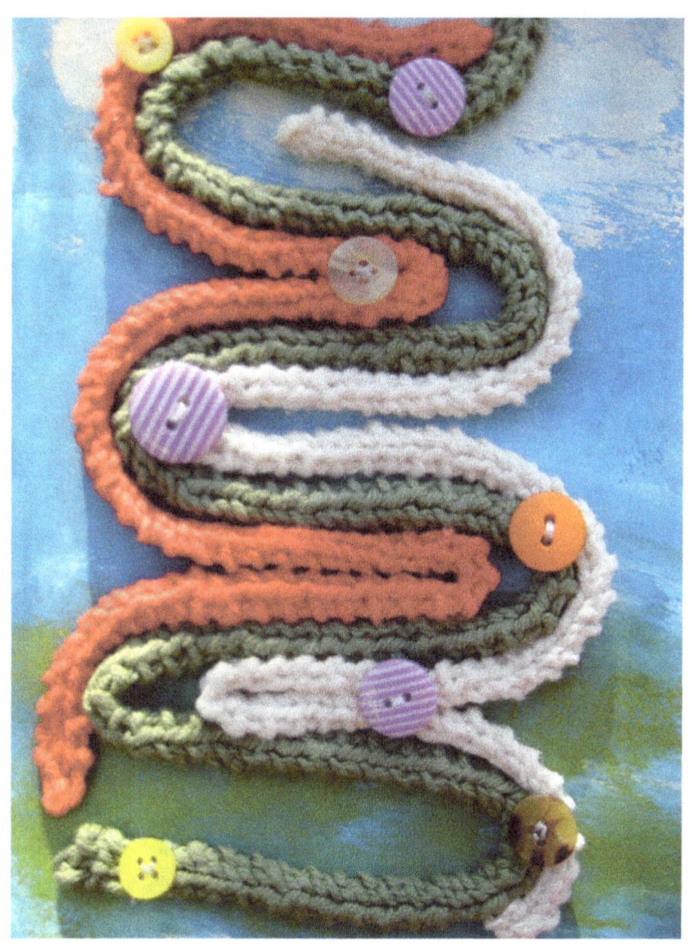

*This card is an abstract solution for the Christmas tree. The idea is three colored bands: Red, "Tropical Leaves" (green) color, and White. By manipulating them, the relief of the Christmas tree was created. Various color buttons resemble Christmas lights.*

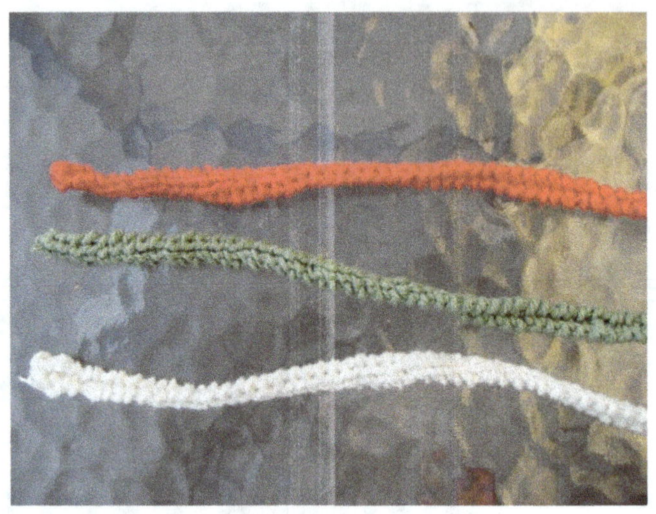

The postcard's base is painted with turquoise acrylic paint that has been randomly added. Sky is tinged with Antique White color and appears faded. The grass was colored using green acrylic paint.

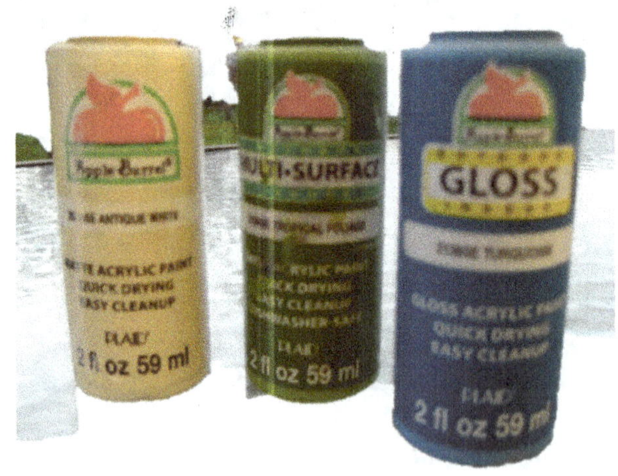

There are two needles required for knitting. On one of them, Cast
on three stitches.

*Row1:* 3K; (3sts)
*Row2:* Sl1, 1P, 1K;
*Row3:* Sl1, 2K;

Repeat 2 -3 rows until you get a bar of the desired length.  After the
knitted piece is finished, the ends of the garment need to be cut off
and hidden in the knit.

Knit three strips of varying colors and lengths, and then glue them on the postcard's surface. A
green strip of "Tropical leaves" attaches the first. The White Stripe is then fixed from the right,
followed by the Red Stripe from the left. Sew buttons in various colors.

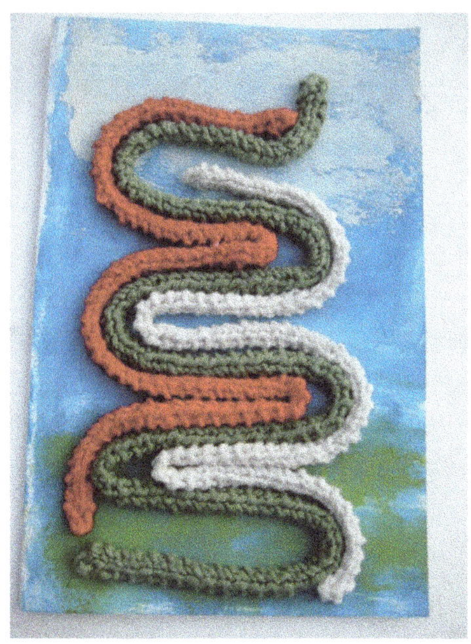 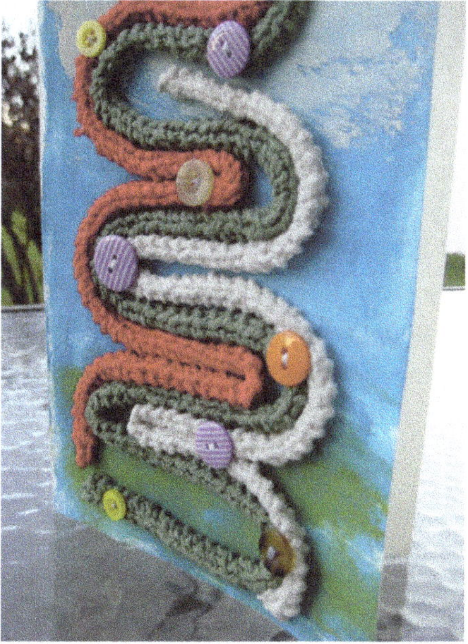

# Mickey Mouse

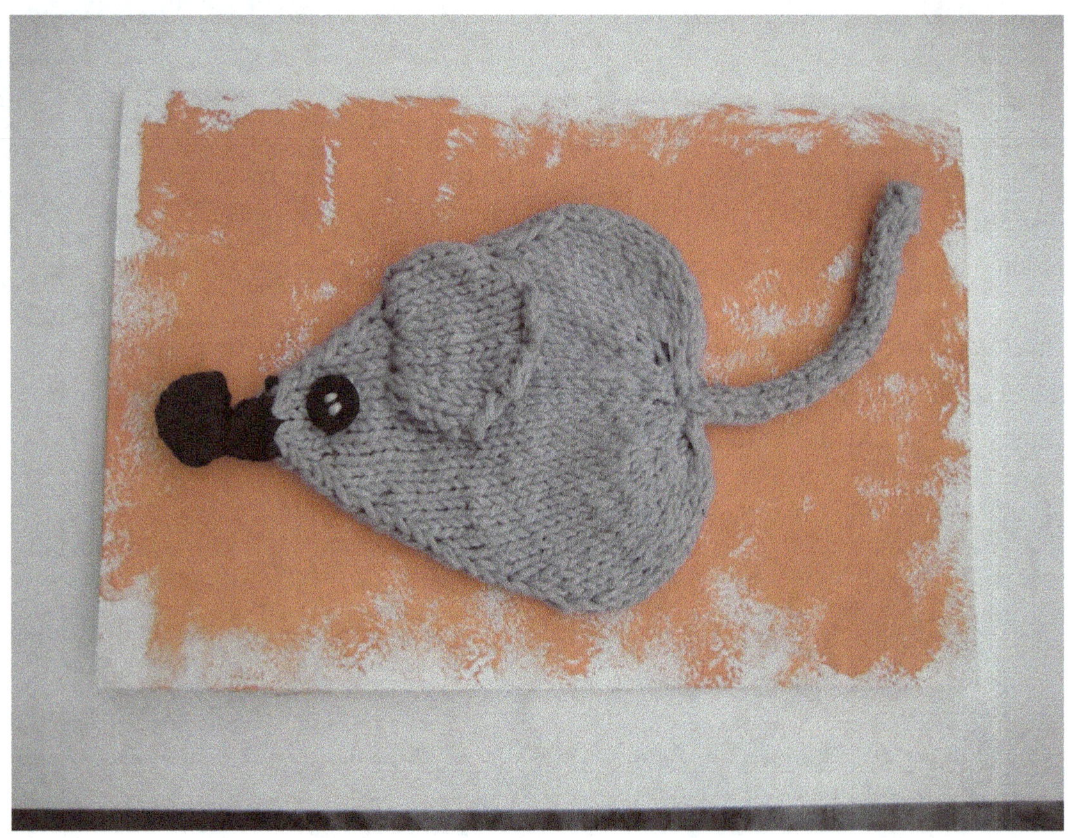

*Mickey is a sincere and loving pet who is looking for a friend. Make this card and you will have a best friend, and you will have a faithful animal who will love you.*

Three knitting needles are required. Knit Mickey in a circle, like a sock in the same direction, without turning your stitches.

You need **Light grey color** yarn.

*Tail*

Cast on 6 stitches.

*Row1:* 3 stitches should be knit and left on the first needle; the remaining 3 stitches should be knit on a second needle.

With the third needle, the garment is joined by knitting in a circle. Keep your stitches straight.

*Row2:* [3K stitches] repeat, (knitted in a circular; first needle: 3 stitches; second needle 3 stitches).

Repeat the 2nd row until you will get a tail of the desired length.

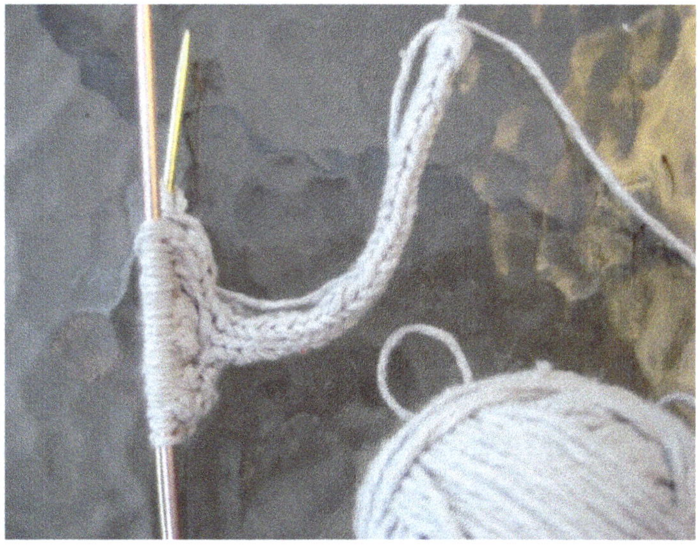

Three knitting needles are needed to knit.

*Body*

*Row1*:[1K, M1, 2K] rep (8sts)
*Row2*:[2K, M1, 2K] rep (10sts)
*Row3*:[1K, M1, 2K, M1, 2K] rep whole row once (14sts)
*Row4*:[1K, M1, 2K; [M1,1K] rep. last parenthesis two more times; M1, 1K] rep whole row once ](24sts)
*Row5*:[1K, M1, 9K, M1, 2K] rep (28sts)
*Row6*:[1K, M1, 2K; [M1,1K] rep. last parenthesis 3 more  times, 2K, [M1, 1K] rep last parent. one more time, 3K.] repeat whole row once (42sts)
*Row7*:[1K, M1, 18K, M1, 2K] rep (46sts)
*Row8*:[1K, M1, 20K, M1, 2K] rep (50sts)
*Rows9- 17*: [25K] rep (50sts)
*Row18*:[K2tog, 21K, K2togrs] rep (46sts)
*Row19*:[23K] rep (46sts)
*Row20*:[K2tog, 19K, K2togrs] rep (42sts)
*Row21*:[21K] rep (42sts)
*Row22*:[K2tog, 17K, K2togrs] rep (38sts)
*Row23*:[19K] rep (38sts)
*Row24*:[K2tog, 15K, K2togrs] rep (34sts)
*Row25*:[K2tog, 13K, K2togrs] rep (30sts)
*Row26*:[15K] rep (30sts)
*Row27*:[K2tog, 11K, K2togrs] rep (26sts)
*Row28*:[K2tog, 9K, K2togrs] rep (22sts)
*Row29*:[11K] rep (22sts)

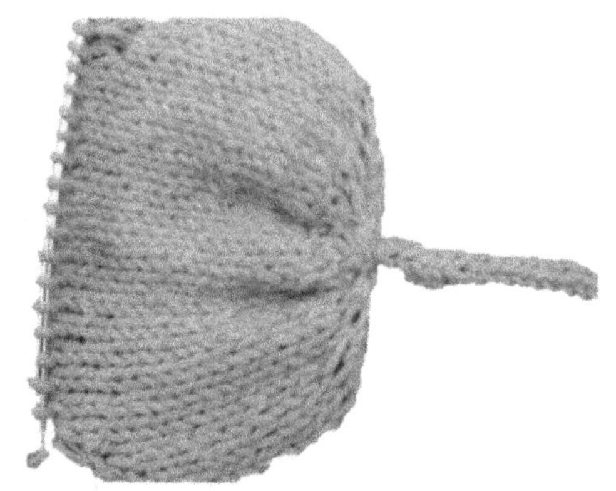

*Row30*:[K2tog, 7K, K2togrs] rep (18sts)
*Rows31, 32*:[9K] rep (18sts)
*Row33*:[K2tog, 5K, K2togrs] rep (14sts)
*Row34*:[K2tog, 3K, K2togrs] rep (10sts)
*Row35*:[5K] rep (10sts)
*Row36*:[K2tog, 1K, K2togrs] rep (6sts)
*Row37*:[3K] rep (6sts)
Attach black yarn after cutting the grey yarn.

*Knit Nose*
*Row1-3*:[3K] rep (6sts)
*Row4*:[K3tog] rep (2sts)
Move the final stitch to the left needle. You have two stitches
on. Use two stiches to knit a big Bobble MB9 (9 stitches).

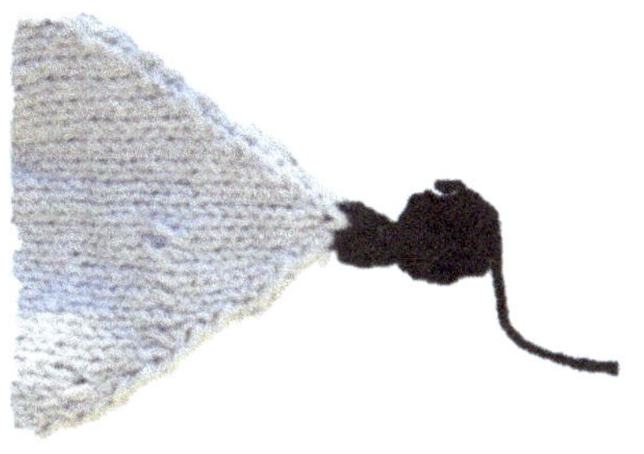

*Ears*

Knit two ears. Use grey colored yarns.

Two knitting needles needed. Knit both sides (Wrong and Right), one at the time. Do not knit
like a sock.

Determine the location of the ear. I picked up stitches in Right upper corner. The ear is an
independent element.

Pick up 9 stitches on the needle. Knit from the right side to the left. Technically, "picking up
stitches" means putting already  knitted stitches on your needle.

*Row1(Right knitting side)*: 9K

*Row2(Wrong knitting side)*: Sl1, 7P, 1K

*Row3*: Sl1, 7K, M1, 1K (10sts)

*Rows 4, 6, 8:* Sl1, 8P, K1

*Rows 5, 7:* Sl1, 9K

*Row9:* K2tog, 6K, K2togrs (8sts)

*Row10:* Sl1, 6P, 1K

*Row11:* K2tog, 4K, K2togrs (6sts)

*Row12:* Sl1, 4P, 1K

*Row13:* K2tog, 2K, K2togrs (4sts)

*Row14:* Sl1, 2P, 1K

Cast off remaining 4 stitches. Cut the yarn and hide the yarn on the wrong side of the knit.

Take a colorless postcard and paint it with "Tropical Orange" acrylic color.

Then wet the knitted garment and let it dry on a flat base. Imitating the eye of the mouse, sew a button. When elements are dry, glue it.

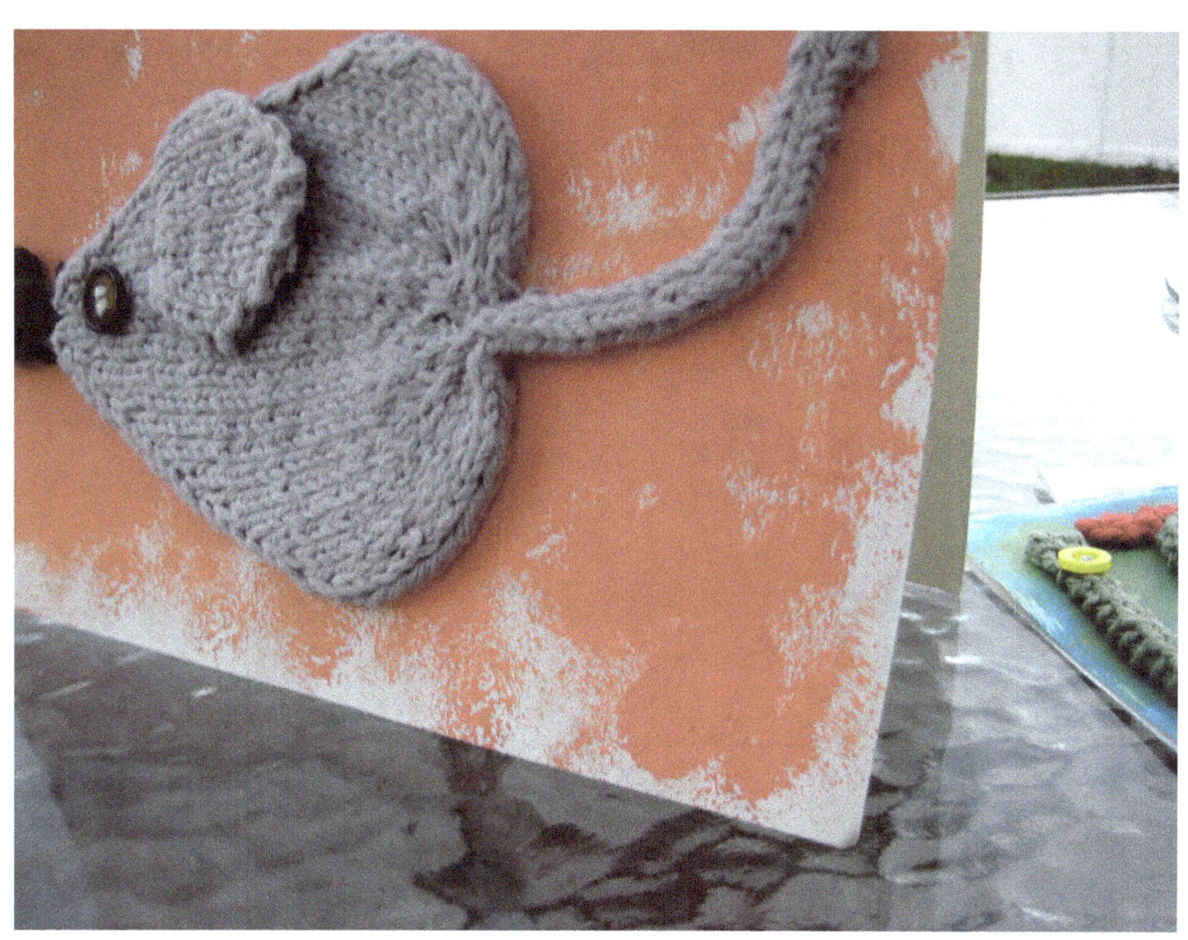

# Flower Arrangements in A Vase

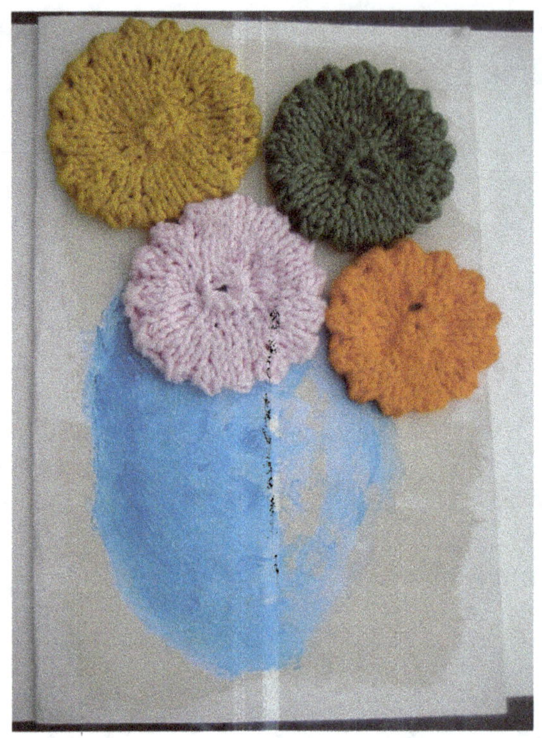

*The pastel color palette of this bouquet exudes coziness and warmth. The soul is inundated with the appropriate emotions as soon as the sight touches the shape and color. Yellowish flowers energize the mind and elevate mood. Greenish flowers are calming and tension-relieving. Pink is a delicate color that represents purity and tenderness. Orange color spurs up fresh, spontaneous ideas and encourages you to appreciate the good things in life. This promotes respect for others and self-esteem. This bouquet is full of favorable thoughts and ideas.*

Paint the postcard with **"Antique White"** acrylic color. Use a sponge to apply white acrylic from right to left. Don't aim for perfection. Color the vase obtaining reflections of both light and dark (dark - the shady and sun-lit sides of the vase). The vase is done using **Turquoise acrylic color.**

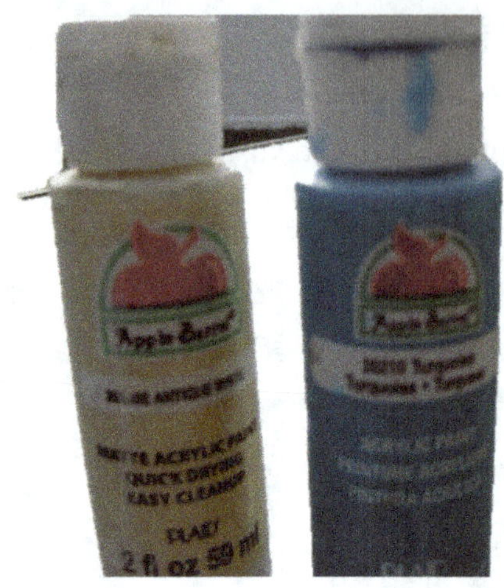

*Knit flowers*. The flowers are knitted in the following colors: **Yellow**, the color of "**Tropical leaves" - Green, Light – Orange** color, **and Pink - Coral** colors.

To knit flowers, three needles are needed. Knit flowers in a circle, like a sock in the same direction. Do not twist your stitches.

On the one needle, Cast on 8 stitches on a single needle. The garment's wrong side is used to knit the item (purl stitches).

*Row1*: 8 stitches are divided on two needles (4 + 4). Knit 4 stitches, leave 4 knitted stitches on the needle which one was used. Use third needle to knit  remained 4 stitches which are located on the second needle. (Two needles has 4 stitches each).

Purling the *2nd Row*, combine the knit in a circle.

*Row3*: [2P, M1P, 1P, M1P, 1P] repeat (12sts continue it in a circle)
*Row4*: P all stitches
*Row5*: [2P, M1P, 2P, M1P, 2P] repeat (16sts continue it in a circle)
*Row6*: P all stitches
*Row7*: [3P, M1P, 3P, M1P, 2P] repeat (20sts continue it in a circle)
*Row8*: P all stitches
*Row9*: [2P, M1P, 3P, M1P, 3P, M1P, 2P] repeat (26sts)
*Row10*: P all stitches
*Row11*: [4P, M1P, 4P, M1P, 5P] repeat (30sts)
*Row12*: P all stitches
When you're done, fold it with the wrong side facing the stitches.
*Row13*: [P2tog, Yo] continue it in a circle
*Row14, 15*: P all stitches

Cast off. Cut the yarn and hide the thread on the wrong side of the knit.

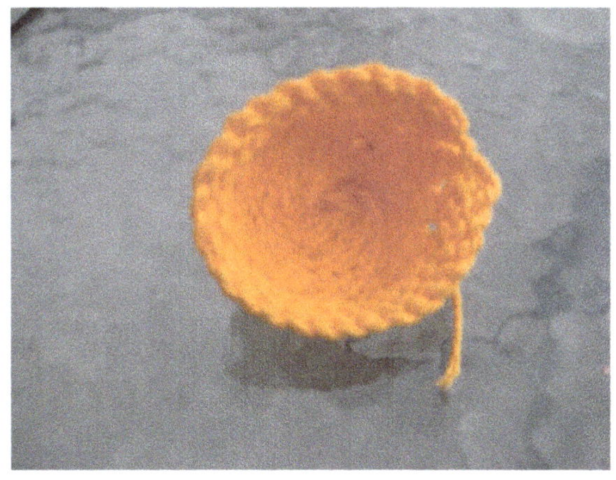
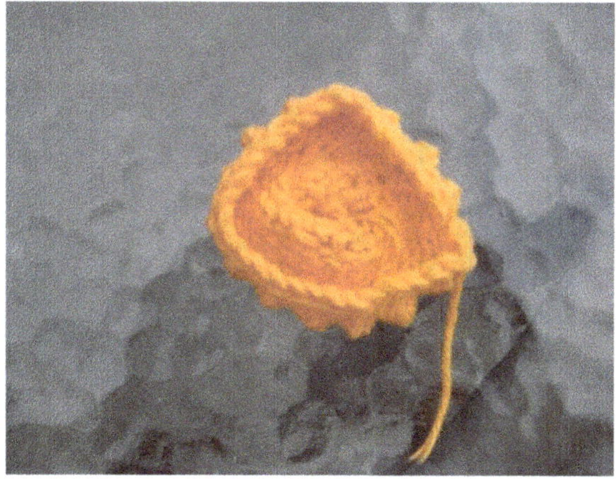

Incorporate the edge into the garment's wrong side.

Stitch it on the wrong side.

After wetting the Flower in lukewarm water,
let it dry.

Then apply glue to the wrong side, glue the flowers.

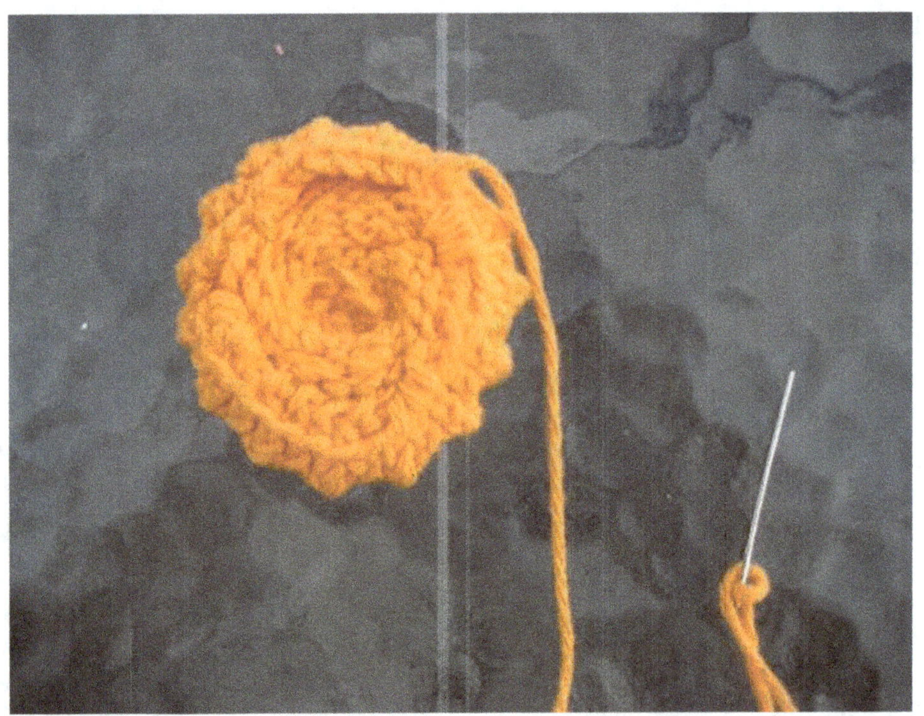

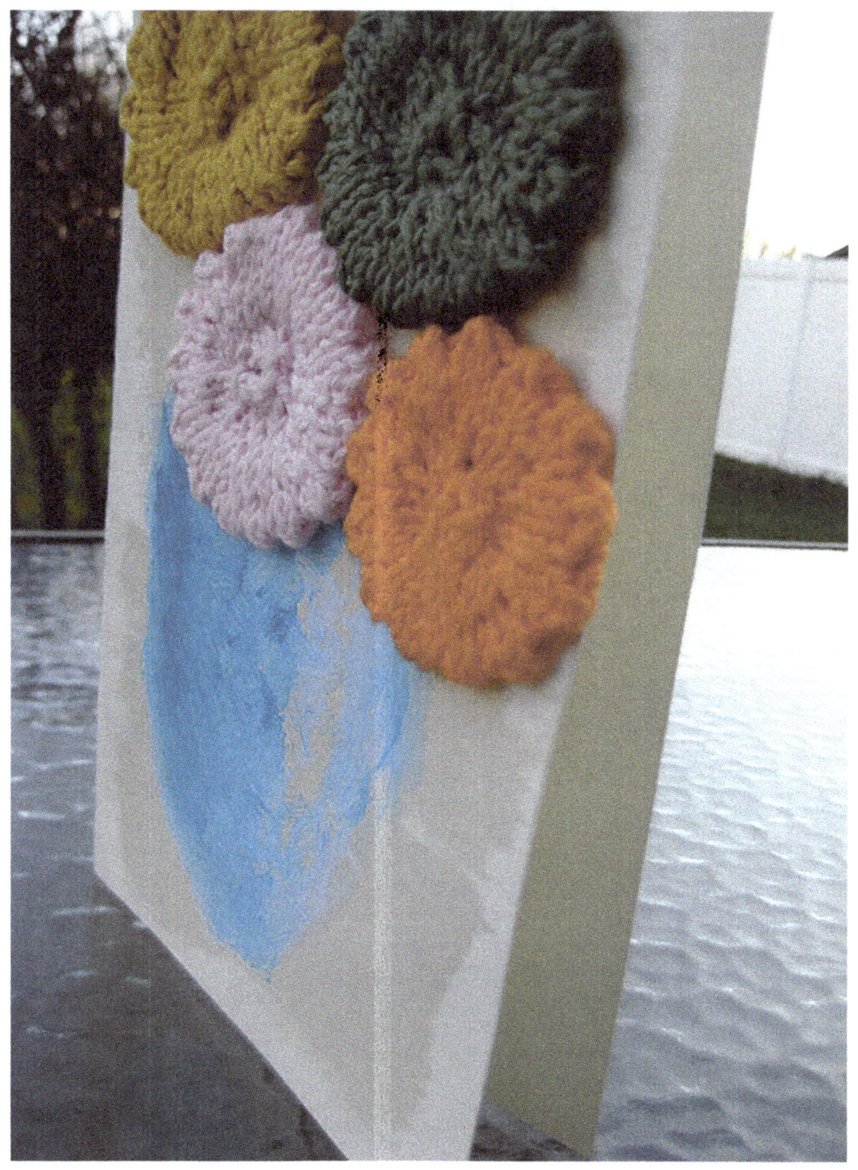

# Birthday Greetings

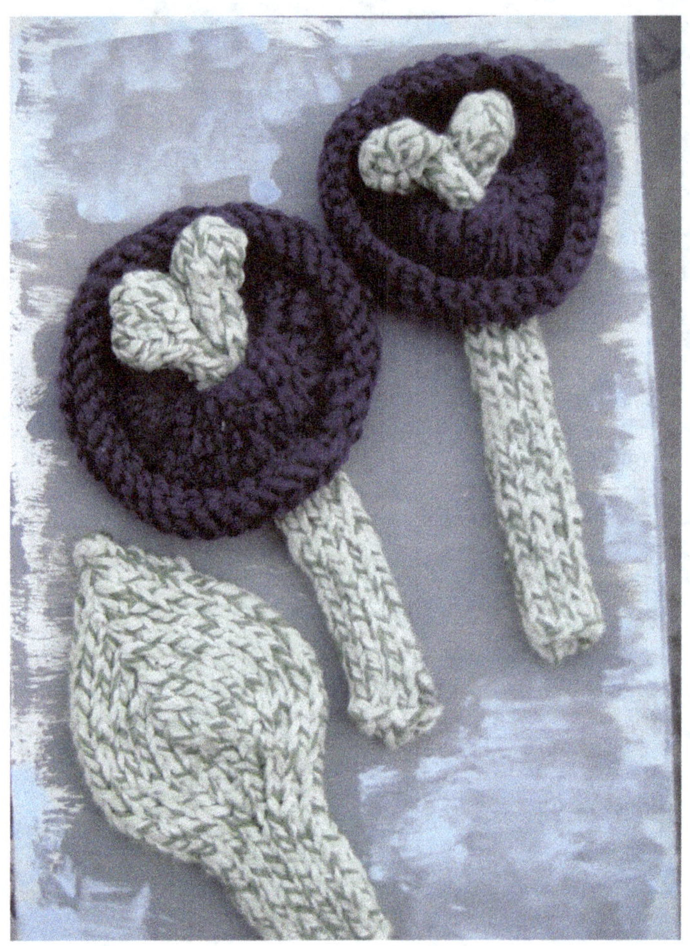

*The day you were born was a special day in your life. Despite the fact that you may no longer recall taking your first breath of air, this day will always be remembered by you. A beautiful ornament, with its long petals, will continue to look fresh and lovely.*

Petals and Stem are the two components that make up a flower. I used **Purple** color yarn to knit petals. The pieces were knitted in a circle, like a sock. Three needles needed. Do not twist stitches on the knitting needle. Knit two flowers, one smaller and the other bigger.

*1st Flower (Bigger)*

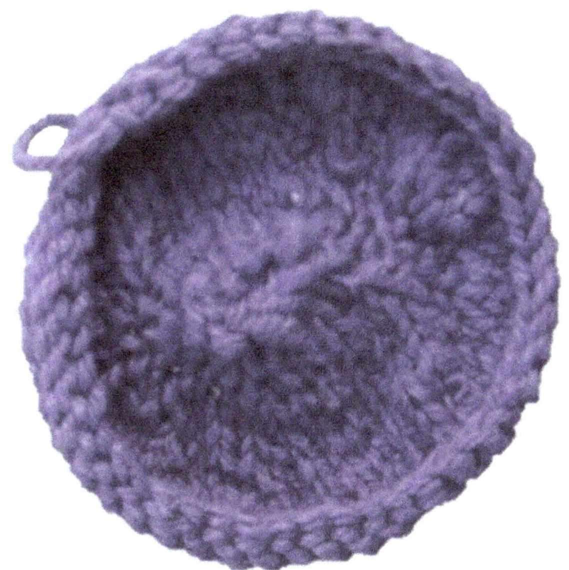

Cast on 8 sts.

*Row1*: 8 stitches are divided on two needles (4 + 4). Knit 4 stitches, leave 4 knitted stitches on the needle which one was used ( do not remove any stitch). Use third needle to knit remained 4 stitches which are located on the second needle. (Two needles has 4 stitches each).

Knitting the *2nd Row*, combine the knit in a circle.

*Row3*: [2K, M1, 1K, M1, 1K] repeat (12sts continue it in a circle)

*Row4*: K all stitches

*Row5*: [1K, M1, 1K, M1, 2K, M1, 2K] repeat (18sts continue it in a circle)

*Row6*: K all stitches

*Row7*: [3K, [M1, 1K] repeat one more time, M1, 4K] repeat (24sts continue it in a circle)

*Row8*: K all stitches

*Row9*: [3K, [M1, 1K] repeat three more times, M1, 2K, M1, 3K] repeat (36sts continue it in a circle)

*Row10*: K all stitches

*Row11*: [3K, [M1, 1K] repeat three more times, M1, 3K, M1, 3K, M1, 5K] repeat (50sts continue it in a circle)

*Row12, 13, 14*: K all stitches

Cast off. Cut the yarn and hide the thread on the wrong side of the knit. Rinke in lukewarm water, lay flat to dry.


*2ˢᵗ Flower (Smaller)*

Cast on 8 sts.

*Row1*: 8 stitches are divided on two needles (4sts + 4sts). Knit 4 stitches, leave 4 knitted stitches on the needle which one was used ( do not remove any stitch).. Use third needle to knit remained 4 stitches which are located on the second needle. (Two needles has 4 stitches each).

Knitting the *2nd Row*, combine the knit in a circle.

*Row3*:[2K, M1, 1K, M1, 1K] repeat (12sts continue it in a circle)

*Row4*: K all stitches

*Row5*:[1K, M1, 1K, M1, 2K, M1, 2K] repeat (18sts continue it in a circle)

*Row6*: K all stitches

*Row7*:[3K, [M1, 1K] repeat 2 times, M1, 4K] repeat (24sts continue it in a circle)

*Row8*: K all stitches

*Row9*:[3K, [M1, 1K] repeat 3 times, M1, 3K, M1, 3K] repeat (34sts continue it in a circle)
*Row10*: K all stitches

Remove stitches from the needle (Cast off).

Hide the yarn ends on the wrong side of the knit, moisten the flowers, and then dry. Put some glue on the knitted element and adhere it to the card.

*Stem*

Three needles are required for knitting the stem.  The mixture of **"Green Lemon"** and **White** yarn colors were used.

On the needle, CO 8 stitches.

*Row1*: 8 stitches are divided on two needles (4 stitches + 4 stitches). Knit 4 stitches, and leave  it on the needle  (do not remove any stitch). Use third needle to knit remained 4 stitches which are located on the second needle. (Two needles has 4 stitches each).

Knitting the *2nd Row*, combine the knit in a circle.

Repeat the second row until the Stem is created. Knit desired length (2 -3 inches long).

The knitted Stem branches out into two distinct portions. Divide the Stem into two pieces, which will result in budding (Bobble). Work on each devided  piece separately. Knit 4 rows, and start making a Small Bobble. Follow directions.

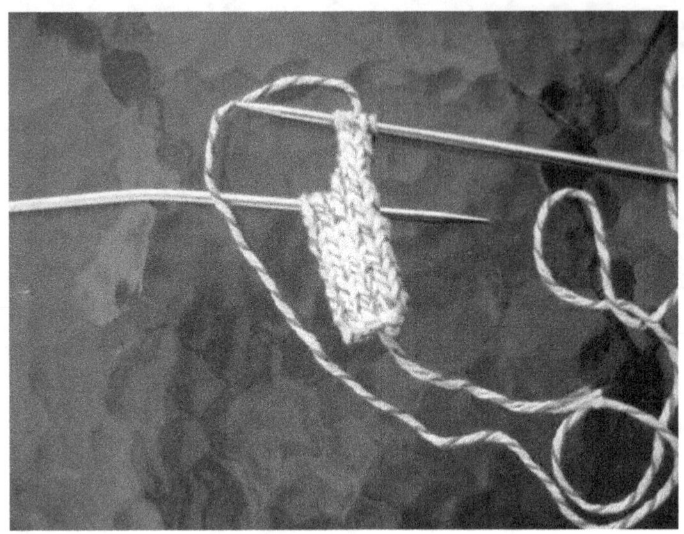

One needle, the fourth, is all you need.

The remaining two stitches on the left needle and two from the right needle are added to the fourth needle. The Stem has been split in a half. Work on Stem (2 stitches +2 stitches) 4 rows in a circle.

*Small Bobble*

*Row1*: [1K, M1, 1K, M1, 1K, M1, 1K] (7 sts)
*Row2 -5*: K all stsitches

Move remained 7 stitches on a single needle.

*Row6*: Pierce the right needle through the seven stitches on the left needle, and make one stitch out of them.

Cut off the yarn, and attach it to the Wrong side (purl stitches) of the Bobble, forming a Bobble.

You have 4 remaining stitches. Knit the second Bobble.

A knitted Stem should be inserted into the Flower's center through a small hole. The Flower and Stem are adhered to the postcard's surface using glue.

*Leaf*

Three needles were used to knit the item in a circle, resembling a sock (double texture). Do not turn stitches on the knitting needles. CO 12 stitches.

*Row1*: Knit 6 stitches  with the first needle; the remaining 6 stitches are knitted with the second and third needle. Join in a circle.
*Row2*:[6K] repeat, (knit in a circle; 6 stitches on the first needle, 6 stitches on the second). You need a third  needle.
Repeat the second row 12 times.
*Row3*: [3K, M1, 3K] repeat (14sts continue it in a circle)
*Row4*: [4K, M1, 3K] repeat (16sts continue it in a circle)
*Row5*: [3K, M1, 2K, M1, 3K] repeat (20sts continue it in a circle)
*Row6*: K all stitches
*Row7*: [5K, M1, 5K] repeat (22sts continue it in a circle)
*Row8*: K all stitches
*Row9*: [5K, M1, 1K, M1, 5K] repeat (26sts continue it in a circle)

*Row10*: K all stitches

*Row11*: [6K, M1, 1K, M1, 6K] repeat (30sts continue it in a circle)

*Row12*: K all stitches

*Row13*: [6K, K3tog, 6K] repeat (26sts continue it in a circle)

*Row14*: [5K, K3tog, 5K] repeat (22sts continue it in a circle)

*Row15*: [4K, K3tog, 4K] repeat (18sts continue it in a circle)

*Row16*: [3K, K3tog, 3K] repeat (14sts continue it in a circle)

*Row17*: [2K, K3tog, 2K] repeat (10sts continue it in a circle)

*Row18*: [1K, K3tog, 1K] repeat (6sts continue it in a circle)

*Row19*: [K3tog] repeat (2sts)

*Row20*: [K2tog] repeat (1sts)

Cast off.

Cut the yarn, then tuck the loose end into the knit. The leaf should be wet with warm water. Allow to air dry. Use glue to attach all elements to the postcard.

The postcard is colored with gray acrylic paint, with small white spaces left around the edges.

Attach the bouquet to the card. Finally, use the acrylic paint **"Spring Sky"** to gently decorate the gray tone of the postcard.

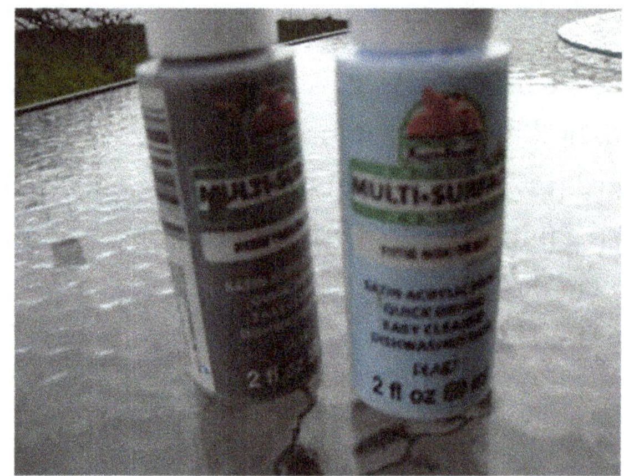

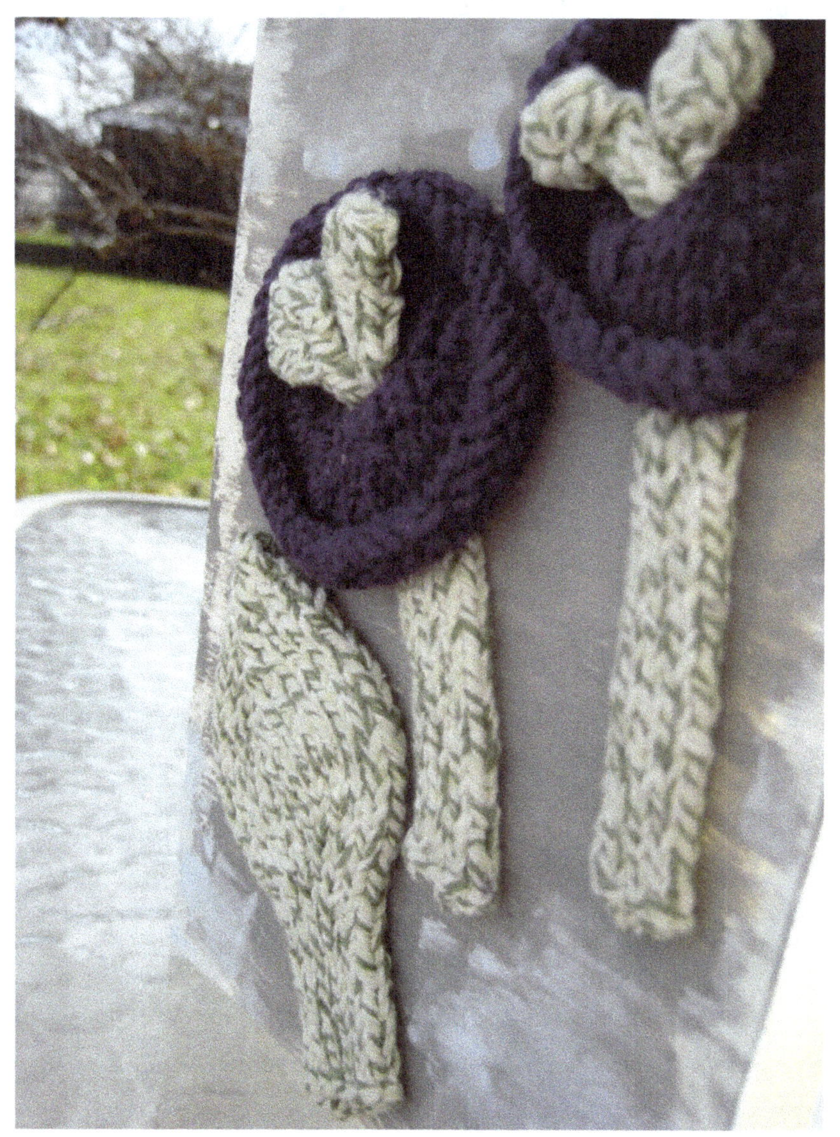

# Blooming Present

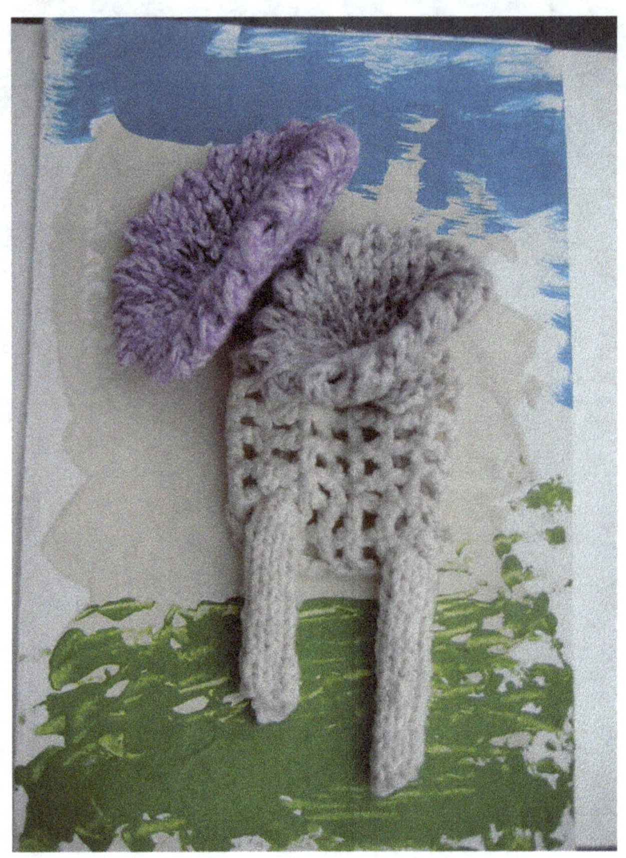

*Flowers are presented to convey feelings, emotions, sympathy. One of the most exquisite examples of non-verbal form is the bouquet, which communicates without using words. The most elegant way to express the deepest emotions is through an arrangement of flowers. The allure of colors, scents, and floral beauty cannot be ignored. Every color has a meaning.*

There are two components of a Flower: a *Stem and Petals.*

*Stem*

**White** cotton yarn and three needles are needed. Using a single needle, CO 6 stitches. Cast 6 stitches on one needle.

*Row1:*3K and leave on the first needle, 3 stitches to be knitted with the second needle and left on the second needle.

A third needle joins the knit. Knit in a circle. Do not twist your stitches.

*Row2:*[3K] repeat; knit in a circle. Three stitches on the first needle and three stitches on the second. Join it not leaving holes.

Knit the flower's stem to the desired length by repeating the second row.

**Light Gray** and **White Mélange** cotton yarns are required to knit petals.

Attach the melange thread after cutting the white thread. The wrong side of garment (purl stitches) is used for knitting.

*1ˢᵗ Flower* White Mélange

You have 6 stitches on the both needles.
*Row1*: [1P, M1P 1P, M1P, 1P] repeat (10sts continue it in a circle)
*Row2*: P all stitches
*Row3*: [2P, M1P, 2P, M1P, 1P] repeat (14sts continue it in a circle)
*Row4*: P all stitches
*Row5*: [2P, M1P, 2P, M1P, 3P] repeat (18sts continue it in a circle)

*Row6*: P all stitches

*Row7*: [2P, M1P, 2P, M1P, 2P, M1P, 3P] repeat (24sts continue it in a circle)

*Row8*: P all stitches

*Row9*: [4P, M1P, 4P, M1P, 4P] repeat (28sts continue it in a circle)

*Row10*: P all stitches

*Row11*: [4P, M1P, 4P, M1P, 4P, M1P, 2P] repeat (34sts continue it in a circle)

*Row12*: P all stitches

Edge. When you done knitting the Flower, you will fold the edge to the wrong side facing stitches (purl stitches). It will be the last step. Now follow these directions.

*Row13*: [P2tog, Yo] continue it in a circle

*Row14, 15, 16*: P all stitches

Cast off. Cut the yarn and hide the thread on the wrong side of the knit.

Incorporate the edge into the garment's wrong side.

Stitch it on the wrong side.

Wet in lukewarm water, allow drying.

*2ˢᵗ Flower* **Light Gray** (Bigger)

*Stem*

You need three needles and **White** color cotton yarn. CO 6 stitches.

*Row1*:3K nd leave on the first needle, remained 3 stitches to be knitted with the second needle and left on the second needle.

A third needle joins the knit. The Flower is knit in a circle. Do not twist your stitches.

*Row2:*[3K] repeat; Knit three stitches in a circle on the first needle and three stitches on the second.

Continue knitting the second row until the desired length of the Flower's Stem is achieved. You have 6 (3 first needle +3 second needle) stitches on both needles.

*Row1*: [1P, M1P 1P, M1P, 1P] repeat (10sts continue it in a circle)

*Row2*: P all stitches

*Row3*: [2P, M1P, 2P, M1P, 1P] repeat (14sts continue it in a circle)

*Row4*: P all stitches

*Row5*: [2P, M1P, 2P, M1P, 3P] repeat (18sts continue it in a circle)

*Row6*: P all stitches

*Row7*: [2P, M1P, 2P, M1P, 2P, M1P, 3P] repeat (24sts continue it in a circle)

*Row8*: P all stitches

*Row9*: [4P, M1P, 4P, M1P, 4P] repeat (28sts continue it in a circle)

*Row10*: P all stitches

*Row11*: [4P, M1P, 4P, M1P, 4P, M1P, 2P] repeat (34sts continue it in a circle)

*Row12*: P all stitches

*Row13*: [4P, M1P, 4P, M1P, 4P, M1P, 2P] repeat (34sts continue it in a circle)

*Row14*: P all stitches

*Row15*: [4P, M1P, 4P, M1P, 4P, M1P, 5P] repeat (40sts continue it in a circle)

*Row16*: P all stitches

*Edge*. When you done knitting the Flower, you will fold the edge to the wrong side facing stitches (purl stitches). It will be the last step. Now follow these directions.

*Row17*: [P2tog, Yo] continue it in a circle

*Row18, 19*: P all stitches

Cast off. Cut the yarn and hide the thread on the wrong side of the knit.

Incorporate the edge into the garment's wrong side.

Stitch it on the wrong side.

Wet in lukewarm water, allow drying.

*Mesh/vase*

You need a crochet hook.

Crochet 24 stitch chain. Make a three-stitch chain, skip three stitches, and double crochet in the chain's fourth stitch. Repeat.

Knit the second and third rows in the same manner as the first row.  Make an element long enough.

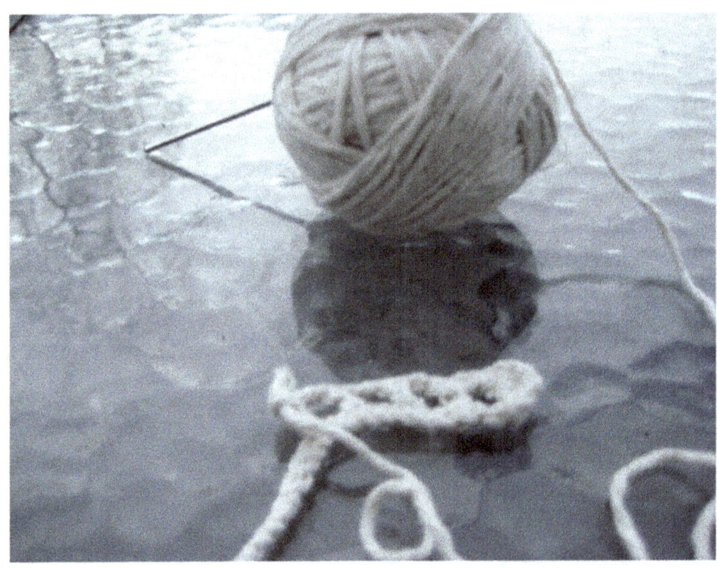

The postcard's surface is heavily painted with a **White acrylic** hue.

The color of the **"Tropical leaves"** is used to paint the grass. The color **Turquoise** is used to paint the sky.

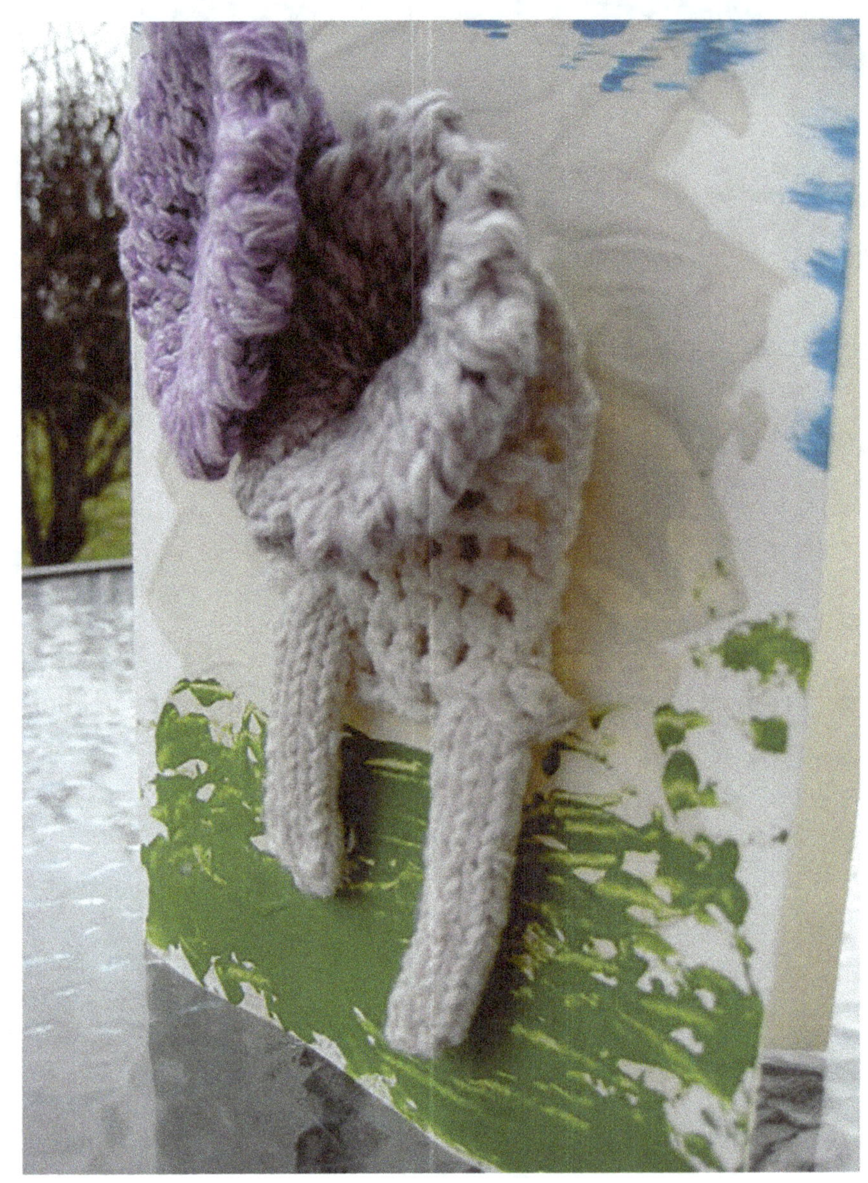

# My House

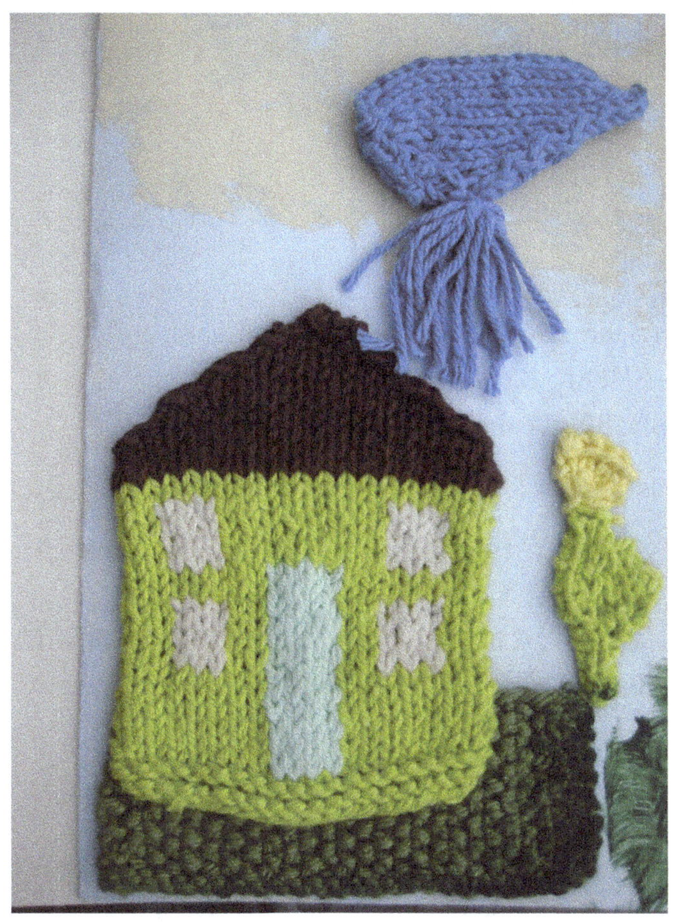

*Home is the place where you feel safe, and happy. This house is knitted from yarns of light colors, full of sun.*

The postcard is composed of many elements like: The House, the Lush Grass, the Blooming Tulip, and the Cloud Hanging in the Sky.

To knit the house, you need **"Green Lemon"** – color **A** - cotton yarn.

Two needles required.

Cast on 22 stitches.

*Row1*: K all stitches
*Rows 2,3:* Sl1, 21K
**B Mint-colored** knitting thread is used to make the door.
*Row 4, 6, 8:* **A color** – Sl1, 8K, **B color** – 4K; **A color** – 9K
*Rows 5, 7:* **A color** – Sl1, 8P, **B color** – 4P; **A color** – 8P, 1K

**White cotton** yarn is used in the knitting of windows - **C**.

*Rows 9, 11:* **A color** – Sl1, 3K, **C color** – 3K, **A color** – 2K, **B color** – 4K, **A color** – 2K, **C color** – 3K, **A color** – 4K
*Rows 10, 12:* **A color** – Sl1, 3P, **C color** – 3P, **A color** – 2P, **B color** – 4P, **A color** – 2P, **C color** – 3P, **A color** – 3P, 1K
Work with two colors.
*Row 13:* **A color** – Sl1, 8K, **B color** – 4K, **A color** – 9K
*Row14:* **A color** – Sl1, 8P, **B color** – 4P; **A color** – 8K, 1K
Join **color C.**
*Rows 15, 17:* **A color** – Sl1, 3K, **C color** – 3K, **A color** – 8K, **C color** – 3K, **A color** – 4K
*Rows 16, 18:* **A color** – Sl1, 3P, **C color** – 3P, **A color** – 8P, **C color** – 3K, **A color** – 3K, P1
*Row21:* Sl1, 21K
*Row22:* Sl1, 20P, 1K

Cut the yarn that was used to knit the house.

Use **color brown – D- yarn** to knit the roof of the house. Attached Brown color cotton yarnt o the knitted garment.

*Row23:* Sl1, 21K

*Row24:* Sl1, 20P, 1K

*Row25:* K2tog, K2tog, 19K (20sts)

*Row26:* P2tog, P2tog, 16P, 1K (18sts)

*Row27:* K2tog, K2tog, 15K (16sts)

*Row28:* P2tog, P2tog, 12P, 1K (14sts)

*Row29:* K2tog, K2tog, 11K (12sts)

*Row30:* P2tog, P2tog, 8P, 1K (10sts)

*Row31:* K2tog, K2tog, K2tog, 6K (7sts)

*Row32:* P2tog, P2tog, P2tog, 2P, 1K (4sts)

*Row33:* K2tog, 2K (3sts)

*Row34:* P2tog, 1P (2sts)

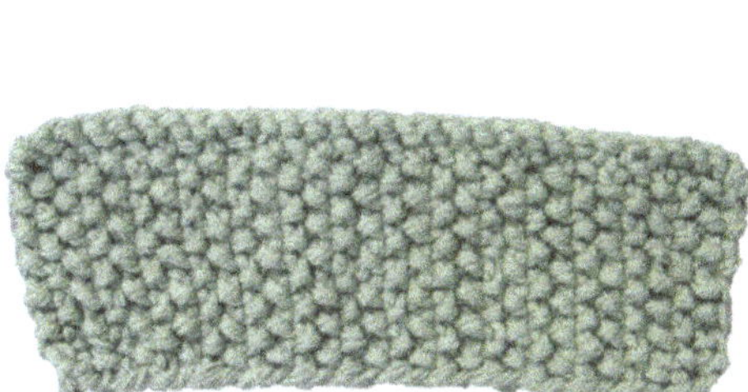

Cast off. Cut the yarn and hide the thread on the wrong side of the knit.

Incorporate the loose end into the garment's wrong side.

You can use any color to knit those pieces.

*Grass*

To knit grass use the color of **"Tropical leaves"**.

Use two needles.

Cast on 30 stsitches.

*Rows 1, 3, 5, 7, 9, 11, 13:* [1K, P1] repeat until you finish the row

*Rows 2, 4, 6, 8, 10, 12, 14:* [Sl1, 1K, P1] repeat

Cast off.

Cut the yarn and hide the thread on the wrong side of the knit.

Incorporate the loose end into the garment's wrong side.

*Tulip*

Knit with **"Green lemon" color cotton yarn.**

You need two knitting needles.

Cast on 3 stitches.

*Rows1, 3, 5:* K all stitches
*Rows2, 4, 6:* Sl1, 1P, 1K
*Row7:* Sl1, Yo, 2K (4sts)
*Row8:* Sl1, 2P, 1K
*Row9:* Sl1, Yo, 1K, Yo, 2K (6sts)
*Row10:* Sl1, 4P, 1K
*Row11:* Sl1, Yo, 3K, Yo, 2K (8sts)
*Row12:* Sl1, 6P, 1K
*Row13:* K2tog, 3K, K2togrs, 1K (6sts)
*Row14:* Sl1, 4P, 1K
*Row15:* K2tog, 1K, K2togrs, 1K (4sts)
*Row16:* Sl1, 2P, 1K

*Row17:* K2tog, 2K (3sts)
*Row18:* Sl1, 1P, 1K
*Row19:* K2tog, 1K (2sts)
*Row20:* Sl1, 1K

**"Green Lemon"** yarn should be discontinued, leaving a tail to be attached to another color.

Attach **Yellow** cotton yarn.

*Row1:* Sl1, M1P, 1K (3sts)
*Row2:* Sl1, 1P, 1K (3sts)
*Row3:* Sl1, 1K, M1P, 1K (4sts)
*Row4:* Sl1, 2P, 1K (4sts)
*Row5:* Sl1, 1K, M1P, 2K (5sts)
*Row6:* Sl1, 3P, 1K (5sts)

Cast off.

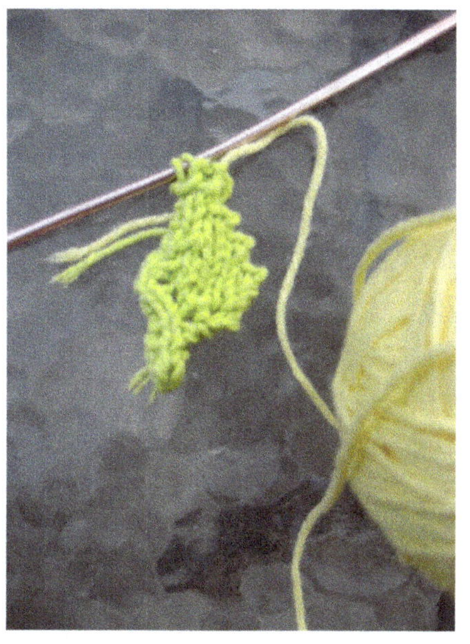

*Cloud*

**"Blue sky"** cotton yarns are needed to knit cloud.

Three needles are needed. Cast on 6 stitches on one needle.
*Row1:*3K and leave on the first needle, 3 stitches to be knitted with the second needle and left on thesecond needle (3 sts first + 3sts second).
A third needle joins the knit.  Knit garment in a circle. Do not twist your stitches.
*Row2:* [1K, M1P, 1K, M1P, 1K] repeat (10sts continue it in a circle)
*Row3:* [4K, M1P, 1K] repeat (12sts continue it in a circle)

*Row4:* [1K, M1P, 1K, M1P, 4K] repeat (16sts continue it in a circle)

*Row5:* K all stitches

*Row6:* [1K, M1P, 7K] repeat (18sts continue it in a circle)

*Rows7, 8:* K all stitches

*Row9:* [1K, M1P, 8K] repeat (20sts continue it in a circle)

*Row10:* K all stitches

*Row11:* K2tog, 16K, K2togrs repeat (18sts continue it in a circle)

*Row12:* K2tog, 14K, K2togrs repeat (16sts continue it in a circle)

*Row13:* K2tog, 12K, K2togrs repeat (14sts continue it in a circle)

*Row14:* K2tog, 10K, K2togrs repeat (12sts continue it in a circle)

*Row15:* K2tog, 8K, K2togrs repeat (10sts continue it in a circle)

*Row16:* K2tog, 6K, K2togrs repeat (8sts continue it in a circle)

*Row17:* K2tog, 4K, K2togrs repeat (6sts continue it in a circle)

*Row18:* K2tog, 2K, K2togrs repeat (4sts continue it in a circle)

*Row19:* K all stitches

*Row20:* K2tog, K2togrs repeat (2sts continue it in a circle)

Cast off

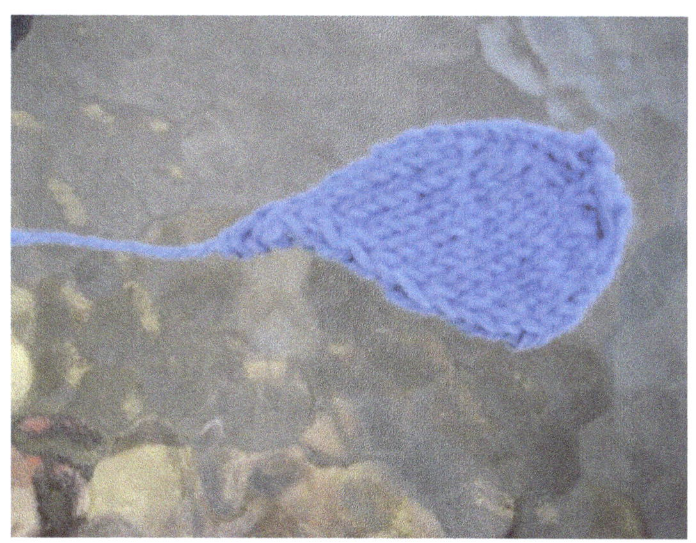

*Fringes/ Clouds rain drops*

A card board is required. Cut the square-shaped piece, size to 2 x 2.

Cardboard should be wrapped in yarn.

- Place yarn end at the back of the card and hold in place.
- Wrap yarn around and around the card over and over. Continue wrapping until you've got a nice, thick chunk of yarn.

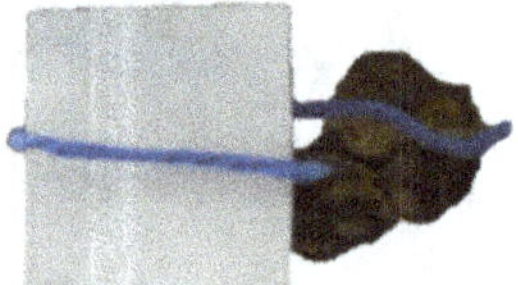

- Cut yarn at one end of the cardboard.
- Match up strand ends and fold them in half to form a loop.
- Put index finger through loop with one hand.
- With the other hand, insert crochet hook from underneath your garment through the opening of where you want to place the fringe.
- Place loop on crochet hook, and pull it down through the opening (careful not to drop any yarn).
- Remove crochet hook, and put your thumb and index finger back inside the loop.
- Grab the yarn ends with your fingers and pull them through the loop.
- Gently pull the ends down until fringe is secured.  This forms a knot at the top of the fringe.
- Adjust fringe and the knot as needed for desired look.

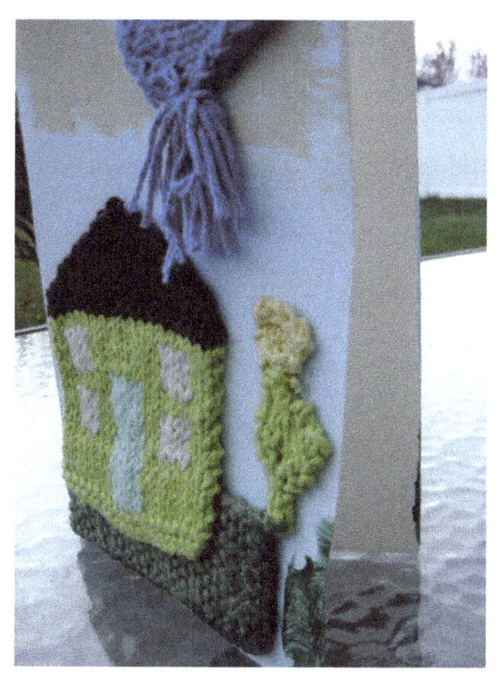

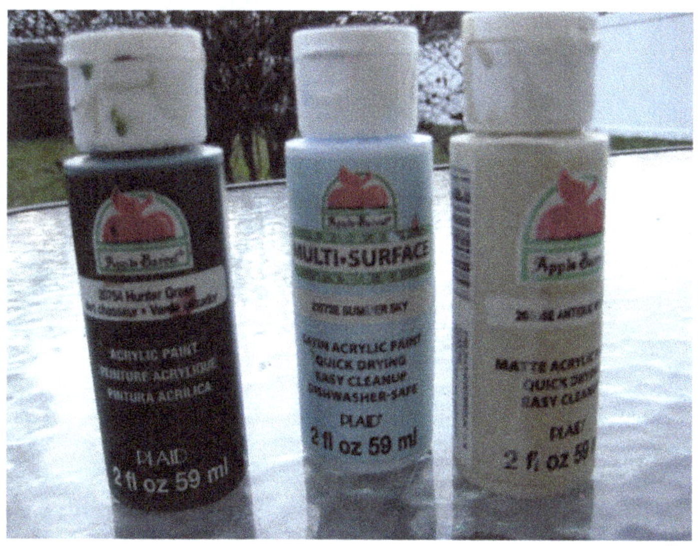
Hunter Green
ACRYLIC PAINT
PEINTURE ACRYLIQUE
PINTURA ACRILICA
PLAID
2 fl oz 59 ml
MULTI-SURFACE
SATIN ACRYLIC PAINT
QUICK DRYING
EASY CLEANUP
DISHWASHER-SAFE
PLAID
2 fl oz 59 ml
MATTE ACRYLIC
QUICK DRYING
EASY CLEAN
PLAID
2 fl oz 59

These hues of acrylic paint were used to color the postcard.

The surface of the postcard is painted with **"Spring Sky"** acryl acid paint. The sky is sprinkled with **White** splatters of longitudinal dashes. The **Green color** is used to paint  the small area located on the knitted grass.

All knitted elements are moistened in lukewarm water. Dried. Glued.

# Bouquet for Mother

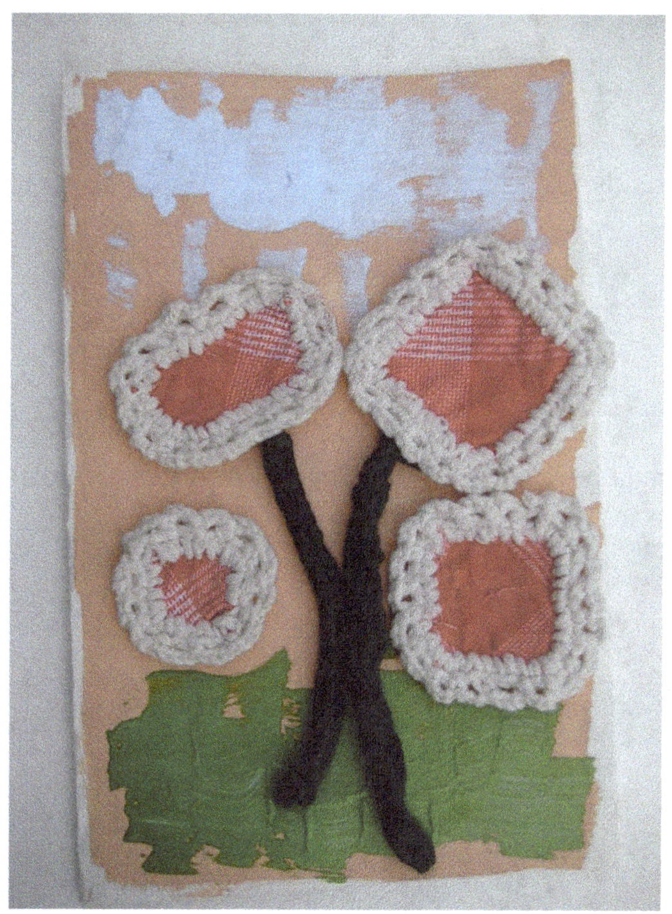

*There is no one better to receive the most exquisite bouquets than your Mother. She is the reason your heart continues to beat and you can see and hear the outside world. Gather all the world's blooms, and set this burgeoning bouquet at her feet.*

The foundation of this postcard is a blue sky with blooming flowers. The flowers' center is made of cotton fabric.  The flower's centre has several different shapes.

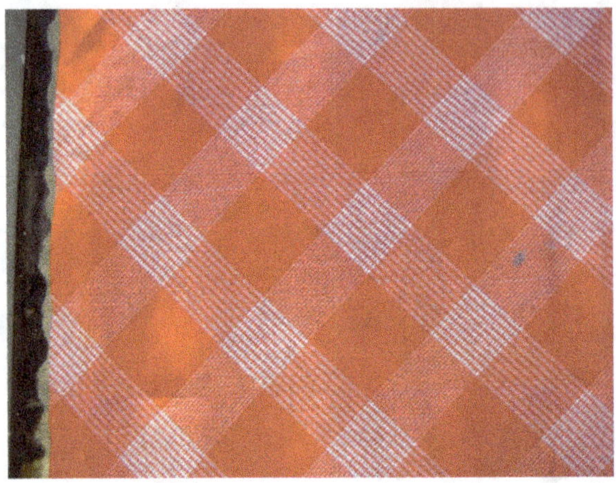

The flower's center might be round, square, or rctangular in shape. Hook is used to knit petals.

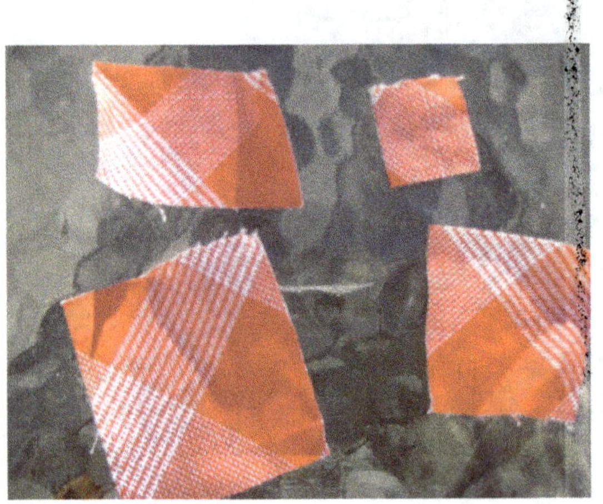

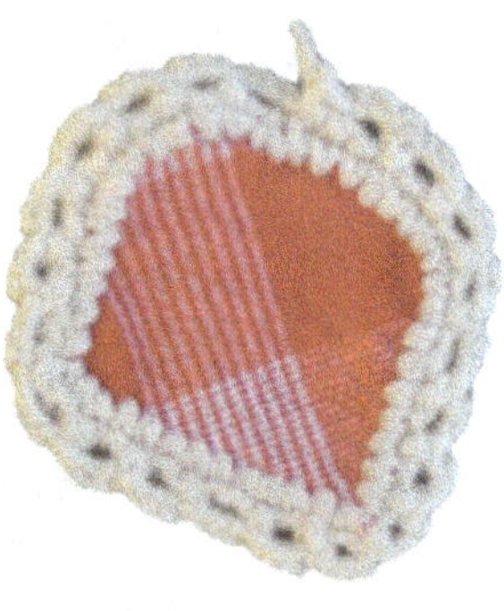

**White cotton** is used to knit petals. Using a hook, punch in holes by hand and make a single stitch. Go around the fsabric.

*Circle 2:* Do not turn the garment, always face RS. Chrochet a chain in 3 stitches. Skip one stitch and crotchet a single stitch into the next stitch. Repeat it going around the garment.

*Stem*

You need 2 needles. CO 3 stitches. **Brown color** cotton yarn needed.

*Row1 (Right knitting side)*: 3K
*Row2 (Wrong knitting side)*: Sl1, 1P, 1K
*Row3*: Sl, 2K
Repeat rows 2 -3.

2 Stems needed to knit. Knit desire length.

The postcard is thickly colored with **"Coral" acrylic paint**, the grass is painted with thick acrylic paint of **"Tropical leaves".** The sky is painted with **"Spring Sky"** acrylic paint.

After coloring the postcard, using glue, attach all knitted elements to the card.

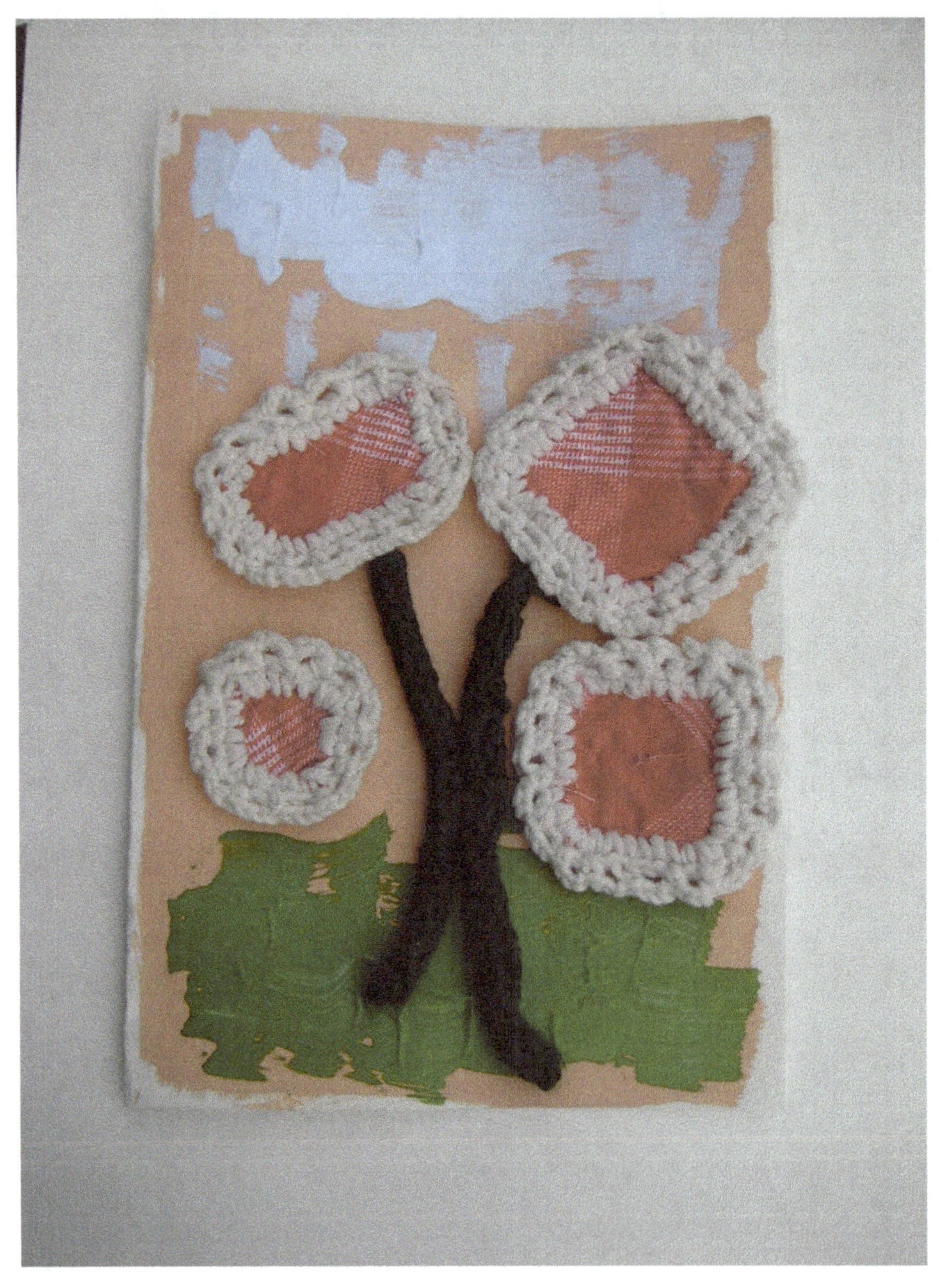

www.ingramcontent.com/pod-product-compliance
Lightning Source LLC
Chambersburg PA
CBHW082359170726
48002CB00020B/2870